Chow Chows

The Owner's Guide from Puppy to Old Age

Choosing, Caring for, Grooming, Health, Training and Understanding Your Chow Chow Dog

By Alex Seymour

Copyright and Trademarks

Disclaimer and Legal Notice

This product is not legal or accounting advice and should not be interpreted in that manner. You need to do your own due-diligence to determine if the content of this product is right for you. While every attempt has been made to verify the information shared in this publication, neither the author nor the affiliates assume any responsibility for errors, omissions, or contrary interpretation of the subject matter herein. Any perceived slights to any specific person(s) or organization(s) are purely unintentional.

We have no control over the nature, content, and availability of the websites listed in this book. The inclusion of any website links does not necessarily imply a recommendation or endorse the views expressed within them. CWP Publishing takes no responsibility for, and will not be liable for, the websites being temporarily unavailable or being removed from the internet.

The accuracy and completeness of information provided herein and opinions stated herein are not guaranteed or warranted to produce any particular results, and the advice and strategies contained herein may not be suitable for every individual. The author shall not be liable for any loss incurred as a consequence of the use and application, directly or indirectly, of any information presented in this work. This publication is designed to provide information in regard to the subject matter covered.

Neither the author nor the publisher assume any responsibility for any errors or omissions, nor do they represent or warrant that the ideas, information, actions, plans, or suggestions contained in this book are in all cases accurate. It is the reader's responsibility to find advice before putting anything written in this book into practice. The information in this book is not intended to serve as legal advice.

Photo Credit: Alisha Bowen of Bowen's Chow Pals

Foreword

Many of the world's top breeders have been involved in contributing to this book, and once you've reached the end, you will have all the information you need to make a well-informed decision whether or not the Chow Chow is the breed for you.

As an expert trainer and professional dog whisperer, I would like to teach you the human side of the equation, so you can learn how to think more like your dog and eliminate behavioral problems with your Chow.

The first Chow Chow I met was Penny, a strikingly beautiful red female and unusually large for her gender. She belonged to an old friend who was returning to town, someone I anticipated seeing often. I can't say I was looking forward to being in the dog's company.

Everything I had heard about the breed made me think of Chows as unpredictable dogs, but Sandy assured me that was not the case. I was skeptical. Sandy made a point of greeting me warmly in Penny's presence, and the dog closely watched my interactions with her human.

As Sandy and I sat and talked in the living room, the dog lay at her feet watching me. The animal's expression was a study in neutrality, but I could have sworn she frowned at me from time to time. Then, I didn't know that the Chow "scowl" is a trademark of the breed.

When Sandy told a funny story that made us both laugh, Penny put her head down and went to sleep. Little did I know the laughter Sandy and I shared sealed the deal for Penny. I had passed the acceptance exam.

Penny was an extraordinarily well-behaved animal, taking her every cue from Sandy. I had the impression Penny watched the human world with tolerance on most days and outright boredom on others. She went everywhere with Sandy, and never once did I see the animal misbehave.

In time, Penny would lie at my feet and accept the occasional pat. She seemed to enjoy conversation more, looking at me gravely as I spoke. I fully expected her to answer me some day. I came to respect that lovely red Chow greatly. She taught me a distinct appreciation for her kind.

When Penny died, I thought we'd have to bury Sandy as well. The woman's grief for her constant and loyal companion was deep and wrenching. That was ten years ago and Sandy has not owned a dog since.

"Penny ruined me for other breeds," Sandy admits. "If I ever do decide to get another dog, it will have to be a Chow, but I'm just not ready yet. She meant too much to me."

The Chow Chow unfortunately suffers from a number of misconceptions that have been perpetuated over the years. In this book, we have involved true experts, many of whom have been breeding the Chow for decades. Quite rightly, they will demystify many of these false myths that continue to plague the Chow Chow.

While this is an exceptional breed with unique and endearing qualities, it is imperative that you understand the things that make these dogs different and what they will need from you in care and companionship before you proceed. That is the purpose of this book.

Acknowledgments

In writing this book, I also sought tips, advice, photos, and opinions from many experts of the Chow Chow breed.

In particular, I wish to thank the following wonderful experts for going out of their way to help and contribute:

UNITED STATES AND CANADA

Tiffany Maddux, Bob and Kathleen Twedt of RHR Chow Chows
http://www.rhrchowchow.com/

Margit and Bernd Lassen of Chow Chow of Peking
http://chowchowofpeking.tripod.com/

Wendy Nieminen & Pete Dingwell of Bearcrest Chows
http://www.bearcrestchows.com/

Zola Coogan of Redcloud Chows
http://redcloudchows.com/

Vancie Drew of Mei-Ling Chow Chows
http://www.meilingchows.com

Odalys Hayes of Kelin Chows
http://kelinchows.com/

Tammy Tosh of Hsot Chow Chows
http://www.hsotchowchows.com

Linda Fernandez of Cherub Chows
http://www.cherubchows.com

Michael & Linda Brantley of Dreamland Kennel
http://dreamlandkennel.com/

Minnie & Paul Odenkirchen of Mi Pao Kennels
http://www.mipao.com/

Caryl Myers of Cejam Chows
http://www.cejamchows.com/

Alisha Bowen of Bowen's Chow Pals
http://www.bowenschowpals.com

Cathy Clapp of FlamingStar Chows
http://www.flamingstarchows.com

UNITED KINGDOM

Pam Godber of Lechan Chows
http://www.lechanchows.com

Chris Clucas of Hiswin Chows
http://www.hiswinchows.co.uk/

SOUTH AFRICA

Bernice Leroy of Ciao Chows
http://ciaochows.co.za/

Table of Contents

Table of Contents

Table of Contents

Table of Contents

Table of Contents

Chapter 1 – Meet the Chow Chow

The Chow Chow labors under a unique myth. All dogs are descended from wolves, but a widely held belief suggests the Chow traces his origin to an extinct bear species. The breed's heavy round features help to explain this assumption. They do strongly resemble bear cubs.

Adherents of the bear theory, however, point to more than appearance. Chows have blue tongues, a somewhat stilted way of walking, and a unique effect on other dogs. Any breed that comes into contact with a Chow immediately looks away or prepares to go on the offensive. It seems as if other dogs are making the statement, "You are not one of us."

Certainly the Chow has a unique demeanor. Bright and intensely loyal to their masters, these aloof, serious dogs thrive on routine. They gaze out at the world with studied and quiet dignity and are reserved around strangers. As a result, the breed can be fiercely protective of both people and property, and has a reputation for aggression that is not wholly deserved. Chows do best when kept by experienced, loving dog owners.

Here is a great story from Linda Fernandez of Cherub Chows, which I think pretty much sums up the Chow Chow:

"Chows are beautiful dogs and so very loyal. My Chows don't take treats from strangers; it doesn't matter how good the treat is, they pretend they don't see it or smell it. They often don't even look at the person with the treat. They could care less really. They simply don't take food from strangers. They also won't load or go any place with people they don't know either. They simply refuse to move.

"I sold a Chow as a puppy, and the man said he wasn't a good enough watchdog. He returned him to me when he was two years old. The Chow sat where the guy left him every day for over a month and waited. At the man's house, he had got another breed of dog to go with his older female Chow. She stopped eating and refused to do anything her owner wanted. She sat and growled at the other dog. She lost weight. The guy called me. I had his boy on the front porch and he started crying before I could see the guy's pick up. I knew he was close. The truck hit the driveway and his old girl leaped out and was up my steps in a heartbeat. That was a true reunion and a great ending to what was a somewhat sad tale."

The History of the Chow Chow

Historical accounts place the origin of the Chow in the Arctic region. The dogs migrated to China with barbarian tribes in the 11th century BC. There are accounts of large warrior dogs accompanying the invaders. The animals are said to have looked like lions, had black tongues, and easily attacked and killed humans.

Animals much like the Chow can be seen in Chinese paintings and bronze sculptures. Unfortunately, however, the written record is scant thanks to the Emperor Chin Shih, who destroyed the bulk of the country's literature in 225 BC.

What does remain describes dogs with large broad heads, small eyes, and short muzzles. Their lips just touched, rather than overlapped, accounting for an unusually aloof expression.

The animals exhibited extreme devotion for their masters, and fierce hostility toward strangers. Over time, the dogs were trained as herders, hunters, home guardians, and were also used as a food source. In Chinese slang, the word for something edible is "chow." It did not become illegal to sell and consume dog meat in China until 1915.

In 1780, British seamen brought the first Chows to England. In 1840, newspaper accounts reference the London Zoological Park housing several specimens of the "wild dog of China." A black female Chow, Chinese Puzzle, imported directly from her homeland, participated in the 1886 dog show at the Crystal Palace.

The dog caught the attention of the Marchioness of Huntley, who was subsequently given a Chow by the Earl of Lonsdale. She immediately asked him to bring her more of the dogs when he returned from his next trip to China.

Lady Huntley established a kennel using an imported male named Periodot. Lady Granville Gordon started a second kennel with one of Periodot's daughters, Periodot II. Lady Faudel-Phillips, Gordon's daughter, then became one of the most influential and important Chow breeders in England.

In 1896, the National Chow Chow Club of Great Britain (NCCCGB) formed and drew up a breed standard. The club held its first breed show later that year at Westminster with 54 entrants. The NCCCGB standard remains virtually unchanged to this day and has served as the basis for every Chow breed standard used around the world.

When Lady Gordon died, her daughter, Lady Phillips, inherited all of her dogs. With her own dogs and those left to her by her mother, Lady Phillips founded the Amwell Chow Chow Kennel in 1919 that operated until her death in 1943.

Thanks to the patronage of wealthy and titled fanciers, the dogs grew rapidly in number and quality. The foundation created in the United Kingdom for excellence in Chow bloodlines made it possible for the breed to be recognized and valued around the world.

In the United States, the first Chow to be exhibited at the Westminster Kennel Club appeared in the 1890 catalog. Mrs. Charles E. Proctor, who founded the Blue Dragon Kennels in 1905, bred the first American champion Chow, Chinese Chum. The Chow Chow Club, Inc., the parent breed club in the United States, was founded in 1906. After World War I, interest in the breed accelerated quickly. This development was due to the 30th president of the United States, Calvin Coolidge. He assumed office in 1923 on the death of Warren G. Harding, and he brought numerous pets to the White House, including a Chow named Tiny Tim.

The increase in interest in the U.S. did not, however, lead to the kind of quality kennels established in England. The American market soon became inundated with poorly bred animals that displayed a pronounced trait for ill temper.

Chows became seen in the popular perception as untrustworthy, dangerous dogs that should not be kept as pets, a stereotype Chow lovers have worked hard to dispel.

Notable owners who took a lead in rehabilitating the public perception of the Chow in the second half of the 20th century included Raymond and Valetta Goschall, Joel Marston, Dr. Samuel Draper, and Pete and Howard Kendall, among others. All bred Chows with excellent, companionable temperaments.

As a result, the Chow is now among the most popular of all companion breeds, valued for its intelligence and devotion. The dogs need owners who will take the time to understand their character, but when you can connect with a Chow's unique way of being in the world, there is no finer canine companion.

Breed Characteristics

The rounded, bearish appearance of the Chow has, at times, worked against the breed. Unscrupulous "breeders" that were little more than puppy mills concentrated on appearance over temperament, creating a stereotype for viciousness that real lovers of the breed have long labored to overcome.

Chow puppies really are the most adorable balls of fluff imaginable, but appearance alone should not be your reason to adopt this or any other breed. Chows may not be right for a first-time dog owner, and even those with years of experience want to go into their first Chow adoption well armed with information.

Facial Expression

Chows have a distinct facial expression that is often described as aloof, somber, or scowling. This breed, unlike the Chinese Shar-Pei, should not have excessive loose skin or wrinkling on the muzzle. Neither contributes to the unique expression for which the breed is known.

The look is distinctly Chow, most evident in individuals with red coats, and augmented by facial shading. The scowl is not a sign of bad temper or anger and is in no way tied to personality. Chows just simply look like they're frowning!

Gait

The stifle joint on a Chow's hind leg carries only a slight bend and is straight in the hocks. This causes the dogs to walk with a gait that might be described as stilted or choppy. The animals take short, quick steps without putting the hind legs far forward or backward. Imagine the motion as that of a circus performer on stilts. This doesn't prevent a Chow from moving rapidly. The breed is also known for its stamina and endurance.

Physical Size

On average, Chows weigh 45-70 lbs. / 20.41-31.75 kg and stand 17-20 inches / 43.18-50.8 cm at the withers. Females typically do not get larger than 55 lbs. / 25 kg. All are classed as "medium" in size and should have a very balanced, squared look. For instance, if a Chow stands 20 inches / 50.8 cm at the withers, his body length should also be 20 inches / 50.8 cm. The projected lifespan for the breed is 9-15 years.

Coat Type and Color

There are two Chow coat types, rough and smooth. The longhaired or rough is the most common. Straight, coarse guard hairs cover a soft, thick undercoat. The smooth-coated variety has a hard, dense outer coat. Both are characterized by an offset ruff at the neck that give the dogs their lion-like appearance.

Photo Credit: Margit Lassen of Chow Chow of Peking - one of the rarest combinations, a smooth blue named Chang.

There are five colors: red, black, cream, blue, and cinnamon. In all coat colors except blue, the dog's nose must be black.

- Although "**red**" is used as a blanket term, it's far too limiting for the range of shades seen in Chows. The coats range from rich mahogany to a light gold with white shading on the ruff, breechings, and tail. Without the shading, the dogs are called "self reds," and "shaded reds" if they are present.

  When the puppies are born, they are a kind of mousy brown with a black mask. As the dog ages, the mask fades and the red comes into the coat, generally starting much lighter than the eventual adult tone. The nose should be black with no spotting, and dark eyes are standard.

- Although there's little to explain about a **black** dog, some Chows show silver shading on the breeching or tails. It's also possible for a black Chow to bleach if exposed to excessive sunlight. This causes an ugly reddish "rusting." The puppies are born black.

- Like the description of red, "**cream**" also ranges across tones from almost white through ivory to near butterscotch. Puppies are typically cream at birth, with light tan on the ears and legs. They do not have dark masks, but their noses often turn a liver color as they mature, which disqualifies them from being shown in the USA (non-black nose color is allowed in the rest of the world on a cream).

- **Blue** might be more accurately described as steel gray. Silver shading is often present, and the overall tone may be very dark to a light silver gray. The hairs on the muzzle and legs are generally frosted in a kind of "salt and pepper" dusting. Blues will also rust in the sun and can have brown shading as well. The blue is the only shade of Chow that does not require the nose to be black. Both gray and slate noses are allowed, but not brown.

- The color called "**cinnamon**" or "**fawn**" in the United Kingdom can be anything from light beige tinged in gray or pink to a darker shade that almost approaches a red hue. The coat doesn't reproduce well when photographed and is widely misunderstood. If a dog is a true cinnamon, the muzzle will display a frosted mixture of light and dark hairs. These dogs are often born silver, so they are easily confused with blues. Puppies also have gray masks that disappear as they age. The nose must be black.

Tail

Chows have tails that are thick at the root, tapering to a tip. The tail is carried high and lies against the back, creating one of the most decorative aspects of the overall Chow "look."

Tongue Color

A Chow's tongue and mouth should be blue-black. Pink or spotted tongues are a cause for disqualification in show dogs. The only other breed that has this characteristic is the Chow's near relative, the Chinese Shar-Pei.

At birth, Chow puppies have pink tongues that should have darkened to blue-black by age 8-10 weeks. If splashes of pink remain after that time, the dog will be classed as "pet quality." It is common for elderly Chows to lose tongue pigment as they age. This is particularly true for dogs with cinnamon or blue coats.

Eye Color

On Chows of all colors, the eyes should be as dark as possible and deeply set in the face. Their shape should be almond like. Note that in the United Kingdom, the breed standard has been changed by consensus of the Chow Breed Clubs and the UK Kennel Club to make eyes oval shape rather than almond to help eradicate entropion.

The Chow Chow Puppy

Bringing a new puppy home is fun, even if the memories you're making include epic, puppy-generated messes! Young dogs are a huge responsibility no matter how much you love them, and they take a lot of work.

The first few weeks with any dog is an important phase that shapes the animal's adult behavior and temperament. Every new pet owner hopes to have a well-mannered, obedient, and happy companion.

With a Chow, that goal is easily attained. They are exceptionally well-behaved pets. Even as young dogs, Chows are not destructive. They don't dig. They don't bark, and they are said to be born almost housebroken, they are so easy to train.

The major challenge in connecting with your new Chow puppy is to think of him as being somewhat more like a cat in his temperament. The term "aloof" is used a great deal in reference to the breed, but there are many descriptive words of equal value: independent, stubborn, dignified, and reserved.

A Chow puppy may not enjoy being hugged or handled by children or strangers. Don't adopt this breed if you want a lap dog that will be open to attention from everyone you know. Even with this agreeable and manageable personality, Chow puppies still require their humans to go through all the necessary steps in puppy proofing the house and providing opportunities for socialization.

Chows are not as prone to problems with whining, biting, or jumping as other breeds, but they are strong willed and can be resistant to training. Unless you understand the breed, you will be the one obeying commands, issued by your Chow!

Personality and Temperament

Intelligence has nothing to do with the difficulties inherent in training a Chow. Make no mistake, the Chow is a smart dog. It can take no more than a change in the tone of your voice to correct this breed, but not if he has been allowed to dominate the household from the day he set his paws on the property.

Chows are not driven by the same need to please evident in more amenable breeds like Labrador Retrievers. They absolutely refuse to be forced to do anything, and resorting to any kind of physical punishment is a critical mistake. If you want a Chow to respect you, you must respect him. There is no other way to form a bond with these regal animals.

Socialization is critical to teach the Chow that if a stranger is introduced to him by his owner, and approaches properly and respectfully, that person may be accepted. Never tease a Chow. They won't forget the breach of etiquette, ever.

Chows mind their own business and don't go looking for trouble, but they are territorial, assuming a responsibility to protect home and family they take quite seriously. On his home ground, a Chow will not let a stranger go unchallenged. The dog will not accept a visitor until his master greets the person.

Because Chow puppies are so well behaved and obedient, many people are lax about training their new pets. This is a serious mistake. Never underestimate a Chow's stubbornness, or his ability to take over and run your household. When a cute Chow puppy becomes a rebellious Chow teenager, you'll understand quickly that you have not won your dog's respect and will have a chore on your hands to correct that problem.

Chows do not like to be outside dogs left to their own devices. When you are home, your pet will want to be with you. This is a highly devoted and companionable breed. They will adjust fine to being alone when you are at work, but if denied the human contact they crave, Chows become anti-social and contentious.

Margit Lassen of Chow Chow of Peking adds this about Chows: "I got my first Chow when we moved to Canada in 1977 and had my first Chow litter in 1997. During those years, we experienced all kinds of differences in temperament; we had the very shy one, due to bad upbringing from the breeder, to over-friendly, jumping up at all visitors. We called her our Labrachow, because she was like a Labrador, loving everybody, which is not normal Chow character. But most of them were very aloof with strangers, and it takes a while until they warm up to a new person, which makes it more difficult to rehome a Chow.

With Other Pets

One of the myths about the Chow Chow is that they do not get along with other animals. Tiffany Maddux of RHR Chow Chows tackles this misconception:

"Although most Chow Chows that are well socialized get along great with other pets, I personally find that there can be instances where males, when allowed, can be territorial of their home with other male dogs. Most of the time, proper training and lots of socialization prevent this from ever being a problem. But otherwise, the girls get along quite well and are pretty comical when they play. I also have them around my personal dogs, including a Doberman, Dachshund, cat, and Chihuahua. All do quite well, and I even have my house Chows out with the horses when we let them in the big yard to graze. They never chase, they do investigate, but will walk with the horses without a problem. I have several Chows with families that work farms and say they make great farm dogs.

"I know that Chows do have a bad reputation just like many other breeds, but most everything is fabricated. Yes, Chows are stubborn and do not always like to listen, but this to me is a sign of intelligence and understanding. A dog that follows your every word and would jump off a cliff because you told it to is not a good trait in my eyes."

With Children

Probably the biggest myth about the Chow Chow is that they are dangerous and unsuitable for families!

Photo Credit: Tiffany Maddux of RHR Chow Chows

I'll let some our breeders involved in the book tell you their experiences:

"We have raised Chows for nearly 28 years and probably 89% of our puppies go to families with children, and the Chow does VERY well. They were bred to be family protectors, and this includes children. I actually have a Chow that I sold to a lady that does in-home daycare and the Chow, a big cream boy, hangs out with all the kids and watches out for them. He's never acted badly with any of them. I do agree that training and socialization are key, but to rule out an entire breed as a kid's dog is ridiculous to me. Any dog, regardless of breed, can do poorly with kids, but from my experiences, the smaller breeds are less tolerant of children and more snappy, while a Chow will avoid a situation that makes them uncomfortable."

– Tiffany Maddux of RHR Chow Chows

"I have been breeding Chows for well over 30 years and also a handler and trainer of many other breeds. The Chow is WONDERFUL for kids, and they are great with other animals as well. It is misunderstood about those qualities. I can give you many accounts where they saved my kids. That a Chow needs adults ONLY is another myth. First, it needs to come from a good line, and the key to Chows is they need socialization. Depending on the dogs and the people, they can be a first-time owner's pet as well."

– Odalys Hayes of Kelin Chows

"Chows make wonderful family dogs, and both of my daughters grew up with Chows from the time they were born. And YES, my puppies are very playful, especially with kids! My 4-year-old granddaughter loves to come over and sit in the middle of a litter of puppies and love all over them. She's also helped me bottle feed puppies I have had to hand raise."

– Vancie Drew of Mei-Ling Chow Chows

Do manage your Chow's meetings with all people, regardless of their age, who come into your home. This is a reserved and private breed. Give your Chow a place to stay safely away from gatherings and levels of activity that would be uncomfortable for him.

Personally, I don't think it is a good idea to have ANY dog with children under 3-4 years old. Prior to that, they don't understand pinching, pulling, and grabbing is not OK, and the dog could bite in self-defense. Wait until your children are 4-5 years of age, when they are old enough to understand the Chow Chow's disposition and to respect his boundaries.

Male or Female?

Typically, my position on gender is that it doesn't matter, but given the unique Chow personality, there are some considerations worthy of note.

Males are larger with heavier coats. They are more imperious in their bearing, but under the right circumstances, that can translate as aggression. Females are smaller, have lighter coats, and although they can be high strung, tend to be more laid back than males.

The greatest negative behaviors cited for male dogs of any breed are spraying and territorial urine marking.

Breeders make pet-quality animals available because they do not conform to the accepted breed standard. Such dogs are not suitable for exhibition or for use in a breeding program. Spaying and neutering under these circumstances protects the integrity of the breeder's bloodlines. In addition, reduced hormone levels stop spraying in males and moodiness when a female is in heat, but the procedures do nothing to alter the dog's core personality.

As a breed, the Chow's false reputation for aggression derives largely from unscrupulous puppy mills that churn out litters with no thought to the genetics of temperament. Experienced, professional breeders with a true knowledge and understanding of Chow genetics and personality should be the only facilities to breed these magnificent dogs.

Even with these gender-based considerations, however, it is important to focus on the individual dog, especially in instances where you may be adopting an adult. The real determining factor in any dog's long-term behavior is the quality of its treatment and training. A Chow that has been abused can be a real challenge.

Puppy or Adult Dog?

People love puppies for all the obvious reasons. They are adorable, and the younger the dog is at adoption, the longer your time with your pet. At an average lifespan prediction of 9-15 years, Chows are long lived in relation to their size.

If you do find an adult dog in need of adoption, longevity shouldn't be a "deal breaker" in welcoming the animal into your home, but it is imperative that you understand the circumstances under which the Chow was surrendered.

I am a huge advocate of all animal rescue organizations. The numbers of homeless companion animals in need of adoption stands at shocking levels. To give one of these creatures a "forever" home is an enormous act of kindness. You will be saving a life.

In the vast majority of cases, Chows are wonderful dogs. If your heart is set on one, I understand why. But if you are searching for a loyal four-legged friend of any breed, please do not rule out a shelter adoption.

Regardless of the breed you choose, please support rescue organizations. Such groups are always in need of donations and volunteer hours. When you do adopt a rescue dog, especially a Chow or a Chow mix, find out as much as possible about the dog's background.

You will have to work hard to gain the trust of an adult Chow. Consult with a dedicated Chow rescue group if possible. The volunteers with the organization can guide you through building a relationship with the animal.

One or Two?

When you're confronted with a gorgeous litter of Chow puppies, your heart may tell you to go ahead and get two. Listen to your brain! Owning one dog is a serious commitment of time and money, but with two dogs, everything doubles: food, housebreaking, training, vet bills, boarding fees, and time.

With growing Chows, there is the added responsibility of training and grooming. These dogs must be brushed at least 3 times a week! Yes, it is harder to introduce an adult dog to a puppy in the future, but especially if you are a first-time Chow owner, I would recommend starting with just one.

The Need for Socialization

Any breed, no matter how well regarded for its temperament, can still develop bad habits and become obnoxious. Because Chow puppies are obedient and don't tend to act out, many owners don't begin training them at the proper age of 10-12 weeks of age. Avoid this mistake at all costs! (Finish the rabies, distemper, and parvovirus vaccinations before exposing the puppy to other dogs.)

During formal training, understand you will be in "school" as much as your Chow. Dogs will quite happily get away with bloody murder if they get their paws on a compliant human – especially this independent and stubborn breed.

Your job is to be the "alpha," a responsibility for which many humans are ill equipped without some in-class time of their own!

Famous Chow Chows and Their Owners

Since his first appearance in Europe in the 18th century, the Chow's regal bearing and aloof personality coupled with his physical beauty has made him a favorite of the rich and famous. At one time in Great Britain, it was even considered a mark of social distinction to own one of the dogs. Some of the better-known Chow owners in history include:

- Sigmund Freud
- David Lloyd George
- Calvin Coolidge
- Walt Disney
- Clara Bow
- Georgia O'Keefe
- James Cagney
- Joan Crawford
- Clark Gable
- Elvis Presley
- Sally Struthers
- Debbie Allen
- Martha Stewart
- Janet Jackson

Chapter 2 - The Chow Chow Breed Standard

A breed standard is created to codify all the best traits of a breed to provide a basis by which exceptional examples of the dog may be judged in competition and for breeding purposes.

The following American Kennel Club breed standard for the Chow Chow is produced verbatim for reference purposes.

General Appearance - Characteristics

An ancient breed of northern Chinese origin, this all-purpose dog of China was used for hunting, herding, pulling and protection of the home. While primarily a companion today, his working origin must always be remembered when assessing true Chow type.

A powerful, sturdy, squarely built, upstanding dog of Arctic type, medium in size with strong muscular development and heavy bone. The body is compact, short coupled, broad and deep, the tail set high and carried closely to the back, the whole supported by four straight, strong, sound legs. Viewed from the side, the hind legs have little apparent angulation and the hock joint and metatarsals are directly beneath the hip joint.

It is this structure which produces the characteristic short, stilted gait unique to the breed. The large head with broad, flat skull and short, broad and deep muzzle is proudly carried and accentuated by a ruff. Elegance and substance must be combined into a well-balanced whole, never so massive as to outweigh his ability to be active, alert and agile. Clothed in a smooth or an off-standing rough double coat, the Chow is a masterpiece of beauty, dignity and naturalness, unique in his blue-black tongue, scowling expression and stilted gait.

Size, Proportions, Substance

Size: The average height of adult specimens is 17 to 20 inches at the withers, but in every case consideration of overall proportions and type should take precedence over size.

Proportions: Square in profile and close coupled. Distance from forechest to point of buttocks equals height at the highest points of the withers. Serious Fault: Profile other than square. Distance from tip of elbow to ground is half the height at the withers. Floor of chest level with tips of elbows. Width viewed from the front and rear is the same and must be broad. It is these proportions that are essential to true Chow type. In judging puppies, no allowance should be made for their failure to conform to these proportions.

Substance: Medium in size with strong muscular

development and heavy bone. Equally objectionable are snipy, fine-boned specimens and overdone, ponderous, cloddy specimens. In comparing specimens of different sex, due allowance must be made in favor of the bitches who may not have as much head or substance as do the males. There is an impression of femininity in bitches as compared to an impression of masculinity in dogs.

Head

Proudly carried, large in proportion to the size of the dog but never so exaggerated as to make the dog seem top-heavy or to result in a low carriage. Expression essentially scowling, dignified, lordly, discerning, sober and snobbish, one of independence.

The scowl is achieved by a marked brow with a padded button of skin just above the inner, upper corner of each eye; by sufficient play of skin to form frowning brows and a distinct furrow between the eyes beginning at the base of the muzzle and extending up the forehead; by the correct eye shape and placement and by the correct ear shape, carriage and placement. Excessive loose skin is not desirable. Wrinkles on the muzzle do not contribute to expression and are not required.

Eyes: Dark brown, deep set and placed wide apart and obliquely, of moderate size, almond in shape. The correct placement and shape should create an Oriental appearance. The eye rims black with lids which neither turn in nor droop and the pupils of the eyes clearly visible.

Serious Faults: Entropion or ectropion, or pupils wholly or partially obscured by loose skin.

Ears: Small, moderately thick, triangular in shape with a slight rounding at the tip, carried stiffly erect but with a slight forward tilt. Placed wide apart with the inner corner on top of the skull. An ear which flops as the dog moves is very undesirable. Disqualifying Fault—Drop ear or ears. A drop ear is one which breaks at any point from its base to its tip or which is not carried stiffly erect but lies parallel to the top of the skull.

Skull: The top skull is broad and flat from side to side and front to back. Coat and loose skin cannot substitute for the correct bone structure. Viewed in profile, the toplines of the muzzle and skull are approximately parallel, joined by a moderate stop. The padding of the brows may make the stop appear steeper than it is. The muzzle is short in comparison to the length of the top skull but never less than one-third of the head length.

The muzzle is broad and well filled out under the eyes, its width and depth are equal and both dimensions should appear to be the same from its base to its tip. This square appearance is achieved by correct bone structure plus padding of the muzzle and full cushioned lips.

The muzzle should never be so padded or cushioned as to make it appear other than square in shape. The upper lips completely cover the lower lips when the mouth is closed but should not be pendulous.

Nose: Large, broad and black in color with well-opened nostrils. Disqualifying Fault—Nose spotted or distinctly other color than black, except in blue Chows which may have solid blue or slate noses.

Mouth and Tongue: Edges of the lips black, tissues of the mouth mostly black, gums preferably black. A solid black mouth is ideal. The top surface and edges of the tongue a solid blue-black, the darker the better. Disqualifying Fault — The top surface or edges of the tongue red or pink or with one or more spots of red or pink. Teeth strong and even with a scissors bite.

Neck: Strong, full, well-muscled, nicely arched and of sufficient length to carry the head proudly above the topline when standing at attention. Topline straight, strong and level from the withers to the root of the tail.

Body: Short, compact, close coupled, strongly muscled, broad, deep and well let down in the flank. The body, back, coupling and croup must all be short to give the required square build. Chest broad, deep and muscular, never narrow or slab-sided.

The ribs close together and well sprung, not barrel. The spring of the front ribs is somewhat narrowed at their lower ends to permit the shoulder and upper arm to fit smoothly against the chest wall. The floor of the chest is broad and deep extending down to the tips of the elbows. The point of sternum slightly in front of the shoulder points.

Loin well-muscled, strong, short, broad and deep. Croup short and broad with powerful rump and thigh muscles giving a level croup. Tail set high and carried closely to the back at all times, following the line of the spine at the start.

Serious Faults: Labored or abdominal breathing (not to include normal panting), narrow or slab-sided chest.

Forequarters

Shoulders: Strong, well-muscled, the tips of the shoulder blades moderately close together; the spine of the shoulder forms an angle approximately 55 degrees with the horizontal and forms an angle with the upper arm of approximately 110 degrees resulting in less reach of the forelegs. Length of upper arm never less than length of shoulder blade. Elbow joints set well back alongside the chest wall, elbows turning neither in nor out.

Forelegs: Perfectly straight from elbow to foot with heavy bone which must be in proportion to the rest of the dog. Viewed from the front, the forelegs are parallel and widely spaced commensurate with the broad chest.

Pasterns: Short and upright. Wrists shall not knuckle over. The dewclaws may be removed.

Feet: Round, compact, catlike, standing well up on the thick toe pads.

Hindquarters

The rear assembly broad, powerful, and well-muscled in the hips and thighs, heavy in bone with rear and front bone approximately equal. Viewed from the rear, the legs are straight, parallel and widely spaced commensurate with the broad pelvis.

Stifle Joint: Shows little angulation, is well knit and stable, points straight forward and the bones of the joint should be clean and sharp.

Hock Joint: Well let down and appears almost straight. The hock joint must be strong, well-knit and firm, never bowing or breaking forward or to either side. The hock joint and metatarsals lie in a straight line below the hip joint.

Serious Faults: Unsound stifle or hock joints.

Metatarsals: Short and perpendicular to the ground. The dewclaws may be removed.

Feet: Same as front.

Coat

There are two types of coat: rough and smooth. Both are double coated. Rough: In the rough coat, the outer coat is abundant, dense, straight and off-standing, rather coarse in texture; the undercoat soft, thick and wooly. Puppy coat soft, thick and wooly overall. The coat forms a profuse ruff around the head and neck, framing the head. The coat and ruff generally longer in dogs than in bitches. Tail well feathered.

The coat length varies markedly on different Chows and

thickness, texture and condition should be given greater emphasis than length. Obvious trimming or shaping is undesirable. Trimming of the whiskers, feet and metatarsals optional.

Smooth: The smooth coated Chow is judged by the same standard as the rough coated Chow except that references to the quantity and distribution of the outer coat are not applicable to the smooth coated Chow, which has a hard, dense, smooth outer coat with a definite undercoat. There should be no obvious ruff or feathering on the legs or tail.

Color

Clear colored, solid or solid with lighter shadings in the ruff, tail and featherings. There are five colors in the Chow: red (light golden to deep mahogany), black, blue, cinnamon (light fawn to deep cinnamon) and cream. Acceptable colors to be judged on an equal basis.

Gait

Proper movement is the crucial test of proper conformation and soundness. It must be sound, straight moving, agile, brief, quick and powerful, never lumbering. The rear gait short and stilted because of the straighter rear assembly. It is from the side that the unique stilted action is most easily assessed. The rear leg moves up and forward from the hip in a straight, stilted pendulum-like line with a slight bounce in the rump, the legs extend neither far forward nor far backward.

The hind foot has a strong thrust which transfers power to the body in an almost straight line due to the minimal rear leg angulation. To transmit this power efficiently to the front assembly, the coupling must be short and there should be no roll through the midsection. Viewed from the rear, the line of bone from hip joint to pad remains straight as the dog moves. As the speed increases the hind legs incline slightly inward.

The stifle joints must point in the line of travel, not outward resulting in a bowlegged appearance nor hitching in under the dog. Viewed from the front, the line of bone from shoulder joint to pad remains straight as the dog moves. As the speed increases, the forelegs do not move in exact parallel planes, rather, incline slightly inward. The front legs must not swing out in semicircles nor mince or show any evidence of hackney action.

The front and rear assemblies must be in dynamic equilibrium. Somewhat lacking in speed, the Chow has excellent endurance because the sound, straight rear leg provides direct, usable power efficiently.

Temperament

Keen intelligence, an independent spirit and innate dignity give the Chow an aura of aloofness. It is a Chow's nature to be reserved and discerning with strangers. Displays of aggression or timidity are unacceptable. Because of its deep-set eyes the Chow has limited peripheral vision and is best approached within the scope of that vision.

United Kingdom Breed Standard

The following United Kingdom Kennel Club breed standard for the Chow Chow is produced verbatim for reference purposes.

General Appearance

Active, compact, short-coupled and essentially well balanced, leonine in appearance, proud, dignified bearing; well-knit frame; tail carried well over back. Should always be able to move freely and must not have so much coat as to impede activity or cause distress in hot weather.

Characteristics

Quiet dog, good guard, bluish-black tongue; its distinctive short-striding gait allows it to move freely, never lumbering and with excellent endurance.

Temperament

Independent, loyal, yet aloof.

Head and Skull

Skull flat, broad; stop not pronounced, well filled out under eyes. Muzzle moderate in length, broad from eyes to end (not pointed at end like a fox). Nose, large and wide in all cases, black with exception of cream and near white in which case a lighter coloured nose permissible, and in blues and fawns a self-coloured nose (but black preferable in all cases).

Eyes

Dark, oval shaped, medium sized and clean. A matching coloured eye permissible in blues and fawns. Clean eye, free from entropion, never being penalised for sake of mere size.

Ears

Small, thick, slightly rounded at tip, carried stiffly and wide apart but tilting well forward over eyes and slightly towards each other, giving peculiar characteristic scowling expression of the breed. Scowl never to be achieved by loose wrinkled skin of head.

Mouth

Teeth strong and level, jaws strong, with a perfect, regular and complete scissor bite, i.e. upper teeth closely overlapping lower teeth and set square to the jaws. A solid black mouth including the roof and flews, with a bluish black tongue is ideal. However, some dilution may be evident in the gums of blues and fawns and this dilution may be more pronounced in creams and whites.

Neck

Strong, full, not short, set well on shoulders and slightly arched. Of sufficient length to carry the head proudly above the topline.

Forequarters

Shoulders muscular and sloping. Elbows equidistant between withers and ground. Forelegs perfectly straight with good bone.

Body

Chest broad and deep. Ribs well sprung but not barrelled. The distance from withers to elbow is equal to the distance from elbow to ground. Back short, level and strong. Loins powerful.

Hindquarters

In profile the foot is directly under the hip joint. Well

developed first and second thigh with only slight bend of stifle. Hocks well let down. From hocks downwards to appear straight, never flexing forward.

Feet

Small, round, cat-like, standing well up on toes.

Tail

Set high, carried well over back.

Gait/Movement

Relatively short striding, hind feet not lifted high, appearing to skim the ground, resulting in pendulum like action when seen in profile. Forelegs and hindlegs moving parallel to each other and straight forward. Dogs should always be able to move freely and soundly without any sign of distress.

Coat

Either rough or smooth. Any artificial shortening of the coat which alters the natural outline or expression should be penalised, with the exception of feet which may be tidied.

Rough: profuse, abundant, dense, straight and stand-off, but not excessive in length. Outer coat coarse, with soft woolly undercoat. Especially thick round neck forming mane or ruff and with good culottes or breechings on back of thighs.

Smooth: coat short, dense, straight, upstanding, not flat, plush-like in texture.

Colour

Whole coloured black, red, blue, fawn, cream or white, frequently shaded but not in patches or parti-coloured (underpart of tail and back of thighs frequently of a lighter colour).

Size

Dogs: 48-56 cms (19-22 ins) at shoulder. Bitches: 46-51 cms (18-20 ins) at shoulder.

Faults

Any departure from the foregoing points should be considered a fault and the seriousness with which the fault should be regarded should be in exact proportion to its degree and its effect upon the health and welfare of the dog. Note: Male animals should have two apparently normal testicles fully descended into the scrotum. Last updated: October 2009.

Chapter 3 – Where to Start Looking for Your Chow

When you have moved past the stage of just "window shopping" for a dog and think you're pretty well settled on a Chow, there are questions you need to ask of yourself, and some basic education you should acquire.

Is a Chow Chow the Dog for You?

In the first chapter, I offered some commentary on the Chow personality and temperament. This breed has a long history of living in close association with man. That does not mean, however, that the dogs are effusive with their affections. The Chow is a study in quiet devotion and loyalty. The word "aloof" so often associated with the breed is accurate.

A Chow will not fawn over you, but he will always be there. Although a Chow can be a family dog, it is more likely for the breed to bond inseparably with one person for life. Often, for even the most experienced dog owner, living with a Chow ruins them for any other breed. A Chow is a superlative companion.

He will tolerate other people in his world, even visitors, but only as superfluous placeholders who have no bearing on the point of his existence – you.

The most important quality in a Chow owner is patience. If you take the time to get to know your dog, on his terms, according to the dictates of his philosophy of life, you will have a devoted companion with a rare sense of canine humor. You will never mold your Chow to be what you want him to be, but he may well mold you.

The breed cannot be pushed, and they are completely intolerant of anger from their humans – especially physical discipline. If you damage a Chow's spirit, you may wind up with a neurotic dog with a propensity for unpredictable behavior. You must be firm with a Chow, but gentle at all times. A stern vocal reprimand is all that is needed to penetrate the sharply insightful Chow mind.

Tips for Finding and Picking a Puppy

Typically, the first step in finding a specific type of puppy is tracking down a professional breeder dedicated to the Chow Chow breed. Thankfully, this is hardly a problem with a breed as popular as the Chow. The following tips will help you to make more informed choices during the adoption process.

How to Spot Possible Health Issues

Before the "Aw Factor" kicks in and you are completely swept away by the cuteness of a Chow Chow puppy, familiarize yourself with basic, quick health checks you can make even as you are playing with a young dog up for adoption.

- Although a puppy may be sleepy at first, the dog

should wake up quickly and be both alert and energetic.

- The little dog should feel well fed in your hands, with some fat over the rib area.

- The coat should be shiny and healthy with no dandruff, bald patches, or greasiness.

- The baby should walk and run easily and energetically with no physical difficulty or impairment.

- The eyes should be bright and clear with no sign of discharge or crustiness.

- Breathing should be quiet, with no excessive sneezing or coughing, and no discharge or crust on the nostrils.

- Examine the area around the genitals to ensure there is no visible fecal collection or accumulation of pus.

- Test the dog's hearing by clapping your hands when the baby is looking away from you and judge the puppy's reaction.

- Test the vision by rolling a ball toward the dog, making sure the puppy appropriately notices and interacts with the object.

When you have educated yourself about what to look for in a healthy puppy, move on to visiting breeder websites or speaking over the phone to breeders in whose dogs you are interested. You want to arrive at a short list of potential candidates from which to choose. Plan on visiting more than one breeder before making your decision.

Locating Breeders to Consider

If you do not have a national Chow Chow organization or club in your country, you will be faced with searching for breeder sites online. I will discuss evaluating breeders more fully in the chapter on buying a Chow Chow.

For now, know that your best option is to obtain a dog from a breeder who is clearly serious about their breeding program and displays this fact with copious information about their dogs, including lots and lots of pictures.

Finding advertisements for Chow Chows in local newspapers or similar publications is dicey at best. You may simply be dealing with a "backyard breeder," a well-meaning person who has allowed the mating of two dogs of similar type.

There is nothing inherently wrong with this situation, although I do strongly recommend that an independent veterinarian evaluate the puppy before you agree to adopt it. All too often, however, if you go through the classified ads you can stumble into a puppy mill where dogs are being raised in deplorable conditions for profit only. Chows are a breed targeted by such operations; exercise extreme caution.

Never adopt any dog unless you can meet the parents and siblings and see for yourself the surroundings in which the dog was born and is being raised. If you are faced with having to travel to pick up your dog, it's a huge advantage to see recorded video footage, or to do a live videoconference with the breeder and the puppies.

It is far, far preferable to work with a breeder from whom you can verify the health of the parents and discuss the potential for any congenital illnesses.

Responsible breeders are more than willing to give you all this information and more, and are actively interested in making sure their dogs go to good homes. If you don't get this "vibe" from someone seeking to sell you a dog, something is wrong.

Photo Credit: Tiffany Maddux of RHR Chow Chows

Do You Need a License?

Before you consider buying your Chow Chow, you need to think about whether there are any licensing restrictions in your area. Some countries have strict licensing requirements for the keeping of particular animals.

Even if you are not legally required to have a license for your Chow, you might still want to consider getting one. Having a license for your dog means that there is an official record of your ownership so, should someone find your dog when he gets lost, that person will be able to find your contact information and reconnect you with him.

Although there are no federal regulations in the United States regarding the licensing of dogs, most states do require that dogs be licensed by their owners, otherwise you may be subject to a fine.

Fortunately, dog licenses are inexpensive and fairly easy to obtain – you simply file an application with the state and then renew the license each year. In most cases, licensing a dog costs no more than $25.

The Timing of Your Adoption Matters

Be highly suspicious of any seller that assures you they have dogs available at all times. It is normal, and a sign that you are working with a reputable operation, for your name to be placed on a waiting list.

(You may also be asked to place a small deposit to guarantee that you can adopt a puppy from a coming litter. Should you choose not to take one of the dogs, this money is generally refunded, but find out the terms of such a transaction in advance.)

Typically, females can only conceive twice a year, so spring or early summer is the best time to find a puppy. Breeders like to schedule litters for the warm months so they can train their young dogs outside. Think about what's going on in your own life. Don't adopt a dog at a time when you have a huge commitment at work or there's a lot of disruption around an impending holiday.

Dogs, especially very smart ones like Chow Chows, thrive on routine. You want adequate time to bond with your pet, and to help the little dog understand how his new world "runs."

Pros and Cons of Owning a Chow Chow

Talking about pros and cons for any breed always draws me up a little short. It's a very subjective business because what one person may love in a breed another person will not like at all. I think Jack Russell Terriers are fantastically smart dogs, but they are also the drill sergeants of the canine world. I don't have any desire to give my life over to a dog that will run it at that level. My preference is for more laid back breeds that value quiet companionship as highly as a rousing game of fetch.

People who love Chow Chows should be ready to talk about their good qualities as well as the challenges they pose for one overriding reason – a desire to see these very special animals go to the best home possible where they will be loved and appreciated.

Pros of Chow Chow Ownership

- Loyal watchdogs
- Naturally unfriendly to strangers
- Rarely bite
- Warn with a growl only
- Naturally protective
- Do not require a lot of petting or affection. Will ask when they want to interact.
- Prefer not to be cooed or fawned over

Cons of Chow Chow Ownership

- Independent and stubborn
- Can be jealous of their preferred human

- Harder to train
- Not the easiest dog for first time dog owners
- Will bulldoze right over compliant owners

It is also imperative that new owners understand any medical problems from which Chows may suffer. The chapter on health includes a full discussion of such potential conditions.

Approximate Purchase Price

Prices vary widely. Chow Chow puppies for sale from reputable breeders may cost, at a minimum, $1000-$1200 / £1553-£1864, with Chows suitable for showing or breeding costing up to $3500. Most breeders do not list prices on their homepages. You must contact them to discuss an adoption and the attendant costs.

Chapter 4 – Buying a Chow Chow

For many people who have never purchased a pedigreed dog, the process can seem daunting and confusing. How do you select a breeder? How do you know if you're working with a good breeder? How do you pick a puppy? Are you paying a good price?

Photo Credit: Tiffany Maddux of RHR Chow Chows

Pet Quality vs. Show Quality

First, you need to understand the basic terminology you will encounter to rate puppies that are offered for sale by breeders: pet quality and show quality.

Understanding the difference in these designations is often as simple as looking at the offered price. Good breeders do what they do for one reason: a desire to improve the breed.

When a puppy is not considered to be a superior example of the breed, the dog will be termed "pet quality." For most of the rest of us, even when the supposed "flaws" are pointed out, all we see is a wonderfully cute and exuberant puppy.

You will want a breeder to explain to you why the animal is considered pet quality over show quality, but since reputable breeders don't sell unhealthy dogs, this is not a stumbling block, but rather standard procedure.

Show quality animals can cost three times as much or more, so most of us can only afford pet quality pedigree dogs.

Required Spaying and Neutering

Normally, when you buy a pet quality pedigree puppy, it is standard for the breeder to require that the animal be spayed or neutered, typically before six months of age. Again, the reasons for this policy are clearly tied to the primary reason for raising purebred dogs: improving the breed. However, in the case of the Chow Chow, they are a slow maturing breed taking up to 18 months to fully mature. There are many articles about the risks involved and health issues from spaying and neutering too early. They need those hormones in order to have proper growth.

Wendy Nieminen and Pete Dingwell of Bearcrest Chows explain: "New studies have now prompted new recommendations by medical professionals. Current advice suggests to either wait until after one year of age before neutering or spaying your pup or have an alternative surgery done before one year of age. This alternative would be a tubal ligation for a female or a vasectomy for a male. These procedures preserve the organs necessary for hormone production and are not only essential for reproduction, but in the development of homeostasis, body condition, cholesterol levels, energy levels, urinary continence, muscle tone, cognition, behavior and most importantly, they also play a role in the immune system. The rise in the risk of many cancers in response to the removal of the reproductive organs is evidence of this."

Pet quality puppies are, by their very definition, judged to be inappropriate for use in breeding programs. Also, breeders are very careful to in no way contribute to the activities of unscrupulous puppy mills.

Chow breeders are especially vigilant in this regard since the activities of puppy mills have had such a negative effect on the popular perception of Chows as vicious animals.

Why Buy a Show Quality Puppy?

The most obvious reason for wanting to buy a show quality puppy is a desire to get involved in the dog fancy and to exhibit your animal in organized competitions.

How to Choose a Breeder

Ideally, find a local breeder or one in reasonable traveling distance, although admittedly with the Chow Chow breed, you are not necessarily going to find a breeder on your doorstep. Even if you find a Chow Chow breeder online, try to visit the facility at least once before adopting.

Speak with several breeders and find one that you feel comfortable with. You could very well have a ten-year plus relationship with the breeder. Don't get a puppy just because it is close to you. Expect to drive several hours to get your puppy if that breeder seems to be the right one for you.

Be suspicious of any seller unwilling to allow such a visit or one that doesn't want to show you around the operation. You don't want to interact with just one puppy. You should meet the parent(s) and the entire litter.

It's important to get a sense of how the dogs live, and their level of care. When you talk to the owner, information should flow in both directions. The owner should discuss both the positives and negatives associated with the dogs.

Nowadays many Chow Chow breeders are home-based, and their dogs live in the house as pets. Puppies are typically raised in the breeder's home as well. It's very common for breeders to use guardian homes for their breeding dogs.

A guardian home is a permanent family for the dog. The breeder retains ownership of the dog during the years the dog is used for breeding, however the dog lives with the guardian family. This arrangement is great for the dog because once retired from breeding he/she is spayed/neutered and returned to its forever family. There is no need to re-home the dog after its breeding career has ended. There are still breeders who use kennels, but the numbers of home breeders is quite high.

Wendy Nieminen and Pete Dingwell of Bearcrest Chows explain why they ship their Chows: "In Canada, there are not a lot of breeders and with air travel it allows people to choose their breeder rather than settling for local because they are nearby. And a two-hour flight as opposed to a two day drive is much more beneficial to a pup. I don't think people 'need' to always visit the breeder. It isn't always practical. I always welcome anyone to visit but if some can't, that is fine too."

What to Expect From a Good Breeder

Responsible breeders help you select a puppy. They place the long-term welfare of the dog front and center. The owner should show interest in your life and ask questions about your schedule, family, and other pets.

This is not nosiness. It is an excellent sign that you are working with a professional with a genuine interest in placing their dogs appropriately. Owners who aren't interested in what kind of home the dog will have are suspect.

You want the breeder to be a resource for you in the future if you need help or guidance in living with your Chow Chow. Be receptive to answering your breeder's queries and open to having an ongoing friendship.

It is quite common for breeders to call and check on how their dogs are doing and to make themselves available to answer questions.

Contracts and Guarantees

In the best cases, transactions with good breeders include the following components.

- The *contract of sale* details both parties' responsibilities. It also explains the transfer of paperwork and records.

- The *information packet* offers feeding, training, and exercise advice. It also recommends standard procedures like worming and vaccinations.

- The *description of ancestry* includes the names and types of Chow Chow used in breeding.

- *Health records* detail medical procedures, include vaccination records, and disclose potential genetic issues.

- The breeder should *guarantee the puppy's health* at the time of adoption. You will be required to confirm this fact with a vet within a set period of time.

Warning Signs of a Bad Breeder

Always be alert to key warning signs like:

- Breeders that tell you it is not necessary for you to visit the facility in person.

- Assertions that you can buy a puppy sight unseen with confidence.

- Breeders that will allow you to come to their home or facility, but who will not show you where the dogs actually live.

- Dogs kept in overcrowded conditions where the animals seem nervous and apprehensive.

- Situations in which you are not allowed to meet at

least one of the puppies' parents.

- Sellers who can't produce health information or that say they will provide the records later.

- No health guarantee and no discussion of what happens if the puppy does fall ill, including a potential refund.

- Refusal to provide a signed bill of sale or vague promises to forward one later.

Avoiding Scam Puppy Sales

No one wants to support a puppy mill. Such operations exist for profit only. They crank out the greatest number of litters possible with an eye toward nothing but the bottom line.

The care the dogs receive ranges from deplorable to non-existent. Inbreeding is standard, leading to genetic abnormalities, wide-ranging health problems, and short life spans. In the case of Chows, dogs born under these circumstances have extremely unreliable temperaments and are often aggressive.

The Internet is, unfortunately, a ripe advertising ground for puppy mills, as are pet shops. If you can't afford to buy from a reputable breeder, consider a shelter or rescue adoption. Even if you can't be 100% certain you're getting a purebred Chow Chow, you are adopting an animal in need.

Puppy mills see profit, but give no thought to breeding integrity. Again, if you can't:

- visit the facility where the puppies were born

- meet the parents
- inspect the facilities
- and receive some genetic and health information

...something is wrong.

Identification Systems for Pedigree Dogs

Pedigreed dogs may or may not have a means of permanent identification on their bodies when they are adopted. Governing organizations use differing systems. The American Kennel Club recommends permanent identification as a "common sense" practice. The preferred options are tattoos or microchips.

In the United Kingdom, the Kennel Club is the only organization accredited by the United Kingdom Accreditation Service to certify dog breeders through the Kennel Club Assured Breeder Scheme. Under this program, breeders must permanently identify their breeding stock by microchip, tattoo, or DNA profile.

Since 2016, microchipping is compulsory in the UK for all dogs. All puppies sold have to be microchipped by 8 weeks of age, i.e., prior to purchase by new owners.

Any dogs traveling to or returning to the UK from another country can do so under the Pet Passport system, for which microchipping is a requirement. For more information, see www.gov.uk/take-pet-abroad. All dogs registered with the Canadian Kennel Club must be permanently identified with either a tattoo or a microchip.

Best Age to Purchase a Chow Chow Puppy

A Chow Chow puppy needs time to learn important life skills

from the mother dog, including eating solid food and grooming themselves.

For the first month of a puppy's life, they will be on a mother's milk-only diet. Once the puppy's teeth begin to appear, they will start to be weaned from mother's milk, and by the age of 8 weeks should be completely weaned and eating just puppy food.

Puppies generally leave between 8-12 weeks and are usually weaned before they receive their first vaccines. It is not beneficial for the pup to stay longer, as it can have a negative affect for several reasons. One is that the puppy should not have access to nursing after their first vaccine, otherwise that vaccine is void. Some moms will continue to nurse despite the puppy being on solid food.

In other cases, the mom is too overwhelmed with the size of the pups and the size of the litter and she avoids them. This occurs as early as 6 weeks old and can result in bad behaviors as the puppies interact with each other. Their roughhouse playing becomes more and more imprinted on them, and families could struggle to teach the puppy not to play with children as they do with their litter mates.

Trainers recommend training and bonding begin with the puppies' new families by 8-10 weeks. In addition, pups need to be highly socialized between 8-12 weeks with new people, experiences, and places. This time period is very crucial in developing a well-rounded pup.

How to Choose a Puppy?

My best advice is to go with the puppy that is drawn to you. My standard strategy in selecting a pup has always been to sit a little apart from a litter and let one of the dogs come to me. My late father was, in his own way, a "dog whisperer." He taught me this trick for picking puppies, and it's never let me down.

I've had dogs in my life since childhood and enjoyed a special connection with them all. I will say that often the dog that comes to me isn't the one I might have chosen — but I still consistently rely on this method.

You will want to choose a puppy with a friendly, easy-going temperament, and your breeder should be able to help you with your selection. Also ask the breeder about the temperament and personalities of the puppy's parents and if they have socialized the puppies.

Photo Credit: Tammy Tosh of Hsot Chow Chows

Always be certain to ask if a Chow Chow puppy you are interested in has displayed any signs of aggression or fear, because if this is happening at such an early age, you may experience behavioral troubles as the puppy becomes older.

Beyond this, I suggest that you interact with your dog with a clear understanding that each one is an individual with unique traits. It is not so much a matter of learning about all Chow Chow, but rather of learning about YOUR Chow Chow dog.

Checking Puppy Social Skills

When choosing a puppy out of a litter, look for one that is friendly and outgoing, rather than one who is overly aggressive or fearful. Puppies who demonstrate good social skills with their litter mates are much more likely to develop into easy-going, happy adult dogs that play well with others.

Observe all the puppies together and take notice:

Which puppies are comfortable both on top and on the bottom when play fighting and wrestling with their litter mates, and which puppies seem to only like being on top?

Which puppies try to keep the toys away from the other puppies, and which puppies share?

Which puppies seem to like the company of their litter mates, and which ones seem to be loners?

Puppies that ease up or stop rough play when another puppy yelps or cries are more likely to respond appropriately when they play too roughly as adults.

Is the puppy sociable with humans? If they will not come to you, or display fear toward strangers, this could develop into a problem later in their life.

Is the puppy relaxed about being handled? If they are not, they may become difficult with adults and children during daily interactions, grooming, or visits to the veterinarian's office.

Chapter 5 – Caring for Your New Puppy

All puppies are forces of nature, yet you may find your little Chow to be unusually well mannered and obedient, taking to housebreaking so easily the chore is usually done by eight weeks of age.

This pleasant fact does not, however, absolve you of the responsibility to be a cautious puppy "parent," including puppy proofing your house. Even the best behaved little dog can come up with a big (and bad) idea.

The Fundamentals of Puppy Proofing

Think of a puppy as a bright toddler with four legs. Get yourself in the mindset that you're bringing a baby genius home, and try to think like a puppy. Every nook and cranny invites exploration. Every discovery can then be potentially chewed, swallowed – or both!

Household Poisons

A dog, especially a young one, will eat pretty much anything, often gulping something down with no forethought.

Take a complete inventory of the areas to which the dog will have access. If you are not sure about any item, assume it's poisonous and remove it. Remove all lurking poisonous dangers from cabinets and shelves. Get everything up and out of the dog's reach. Pay special attention to:

- cleaning products
- insecticides
- mothballs
- fertilizers
- antifreeze

Look Through Your Puppy's Eyes

Get down on the floor and have a look around from puppy level. Your new furry Einstein will spot anything that catches your attention and many things that don't!

Do not leave any dangling electrical cords, drapery pulls, or even loose scraps of wallpaper. Look for forgotten items that have gotten wedged behind cushions or kicked under the furniture. Don't let anything stay out that could be a choking hazard.

Tie up anything that might create a "topple" danger. A coaxial cable may look boring to you, but in the mouth of a determined little dog, it could send a heavy television set crashing down. Cord minders and electrical ties are your friends!

Remove stuffed items and pillows, and cover the legs of prized pieces of furniture against chewing. Take anything out of the room that even looks like it *might* be a toy. Think I'm kidding? Go online and do a Google image search for "dog chewed cell phone" and shudder at what you will see.

Plant Dangers, Inside and Out

The list of indoor and outdoor plants that are a toxic risk to dogs is long and includes many surprises. You may know that apricot and peach pits are poisonous to canines, but what about spinach and tomato vines?

The American Society for the Prevention of Cruelty to Animals has created a large reference list of plants for dog owners available at:

http://www.aspca.org/pet-care/animal-poison-control/toxic-and-non-toxic-plants

Go through the list and remove any plants from your home that might make your puppy sick. Don't just assume that your dog will leave such items alone.

Preparing for the Homecoming

Before you bring your new puppy home, buy an appropriate travel crate and a wire crate for home use. Since the home crate will also be an important tool in housebreaking, the size of the unit is important.

Many pet owners want to get a crate large enough for the puppy to "grow into" in the interest of saving money. When you are housebreaking a dog, you are working with the principle that the animal will not soil its own "den." If you buy a huge crate for a small dog, the puppy is likely to pick a corner as the "bathroom," thus setting back his training.

Crates are rated by the size of the dog in pounds / kilograms.

For example:

- For larger Chow Chows weighing up to 70 lbs. / 31.75 kg, the crate should be 36" x 22" x 24" / 91.44 cm x 55.88 cm x 60.96 cm.

(Since even the smallest Chows weigh around 45 lbs. / 20.41, the above dimensions should be considered the acceptable minimum for these dogs as well. Standard cage sizes jump from the 40 lb. / 18.14 kg to the 70 lb. / 31.75 kg range with no intervening sizes.)

Put one or two puppy safe chew toys in the crate for the ride home along with a recently worn article of clothing. You want the dog to learn your scent. Be sure to fasten the seat belt over the crate.

Talk to the breeder to ensure the dog has not eaten. Take the puppy out to do its business before putting it in the crate. There may be whining and crying, but even very young Chows tend to be quiet. If the puppy does whine, don't give in! Leave the dog in the crate! It's far safer for the puppy to ride there than to be in someone's lap.

Try to take someone with you to sit next to the crate and comfort the puppy.

Don't overload the dog's senses with too many people. No matter how excited the kids may be at the prospect of a new puppy, leave the children back at the house. The trip home needs to be calm and quiet. Do not overwhelm a puppy with too much attention from the moment it leaves the breeder.

As soon as you arrive home, take the puppy to a patch of grass outside to relieve himself. Immediately begin encouraging him for doing so. Chows catch on very quickly to what is expected of them. Positive and consistent praise is an important part of housebreaking.

Because the breed is naturally reserved, a Chow can easily be overwhelmed in new surroundings and become even more standoffish. Stick with the usual feeding schedule, and use the same kind of food the dog has been receiving.

Create a designated "puppy safe" area in the house. Give the puppy his privacy and let him explore on his own. Don't isolate the little dog, but don't crowd him either.

Photo Credit: Zola Coogan of Redcloud Chows

Give the dog soft pieces of worn clothing to further familiarize him with your scent. Leave a radio playing at a low volume for "company." At night you may opt to give the baby a well-wrapped warm water bottle, but put the dog in its crate and do not bring it to bed with you.

I realize that last bit may sound all but impossible, but if you want a crate-trained dog, you have to start from day one. Chows actually do not like to be made to sleep apart from their humans, but you may be able to at least strike a compromise of having the crate in your bedroom. It's much, much harder to get a dog used to sleeping overnight in his crate after any time in the bed with you.

The Importance of the Crate

The crate plays an important role in your dog's life. Don't think of its use as "imprisoning" your Chow. The dog sees the crate as a den and will retreat to it for safety, security, and privacy. Dogs often go to their crates just to enjoy quiet time, and this is definitely behavior you will see in your Chow.

When you accustom your dog to a crate as a puppy, you get ahead of issues of separation anxiety and prepare your pet to do well with travel. The crate also plays an important role in housebreaking, a topic we will discuss shortly.

Never rush crate training. Don't lose your temper or show frustration. On every aspect of training your Chow, remaining patient is critically important. The dog must go into the crate on its own. Begin by leaving the door open. Tie it in place so it does not slam shut on accident. Give your puppy a treat each time he goes inside. Reinforce his good behavior with verbal praise. Never use the crate as punishment. Proper use of the crate gives both you and your Chow peace of mind.

Take It Slow With the Children

If you have children, talk to them before the puppy arrives.

Explain that Chows have a very special way of being in the world. They are quiet dogs that have to get used to people. The initial transition is important. Supervise all interactions for everyone's safety and comfort.

Help children understand how to handle the puppy and to carry it safely. Limit playtime until everyone gets to know each other. Your Chow puppy will play with your children, but first he has to become familiar with his surroundings and learn who is part of the family.

'Introductions' With Other Pets

Introductions with other pets, especially with cats, often boil down to matters of territoriality. All dogs, by nature, defend their territory against intruders. This instinct is strong in Chows.

As a general rule of thumb, Chows do better with other animals with which they have been raised – both dogs and cats. For the first "meeting," create a neutral and controlled interaction under a closed bathroom door first.

Since cats are "weaponized" with an array of razor sharp claws, Fluffy can quickly put a puppy in his place, but a Chow will remember a first meeting gone bad for life. Oversee the first "in-person" meeting, but don't overreact. Let the animals sort it out.

Since Chows are sometimes described as being very cat-like themselves, the reserved behavior of puppies often stands them in good stead with the family feline. The cat interprets the aloofness as good manners.

With other dogs in the house, you may want a more hands-on

approach to the first "meet and greet." Always have two people present to control each dog. Make the introduction in a place that the older dog does not regard as "his." Even if the two dogs are going to be living in the same house, let them meet in neutral territory.

Keep your tone and demeanor calm, friendly, and happy. Let the dogs conduct the usual "sniff test," but don't let it go on for too long. Either dog may consider lengthy sniffing to be aggression.

Puppies may not yet understand the behavior of an adult dog and can be absolute little pests, but again, the Chow's natural reserve is hugely to their benefit and yours in such a situation. If the puppy does get too "familiar," do not scold the older dog for issuing a warning snarl or growl. A well-socialized older dog won't be displaying aggression with this reaction. He's just putting junior in his place and establishing the hierarchy of the pack.

Be careful when you bring a new dog into the house not to neglect the older dog. Also be sure to spend time with him away from the puppy to assure your existing pet that your bond with him is strong and intact.

Exercise caution at mealtimes. Feed your pets in separate bowls so there is no perceived competition for food. (This is also a good policy to follow when introducing your puppy to the family cat.)

What Can I Do to Make My Chow Chow Love Me?

From the moment you bring your Chow Chow dog home, every minute you spend with him is an opportunity to bond. The earlier you start working with your dog, the more quickly that bond will grow and the closer you and your Chow will become.

While simply spending time with your Chow Chow will encourage the growth of that bond, there are a few things you can do to purposefully build your bond with your dog. Some of these things include:

• Taking your Chow Chow for daily walks, during which you frequently stop to pet and talk to your dog.

• Engaging your Chow Chow in games like fetch and hide-and-seek to encourage interaction.

• Interacting with your dog through daily training sessions – teach your dog to pay attention when you say his name.

• Being calm and consistent when training your dog – always use positive reinforcement rather than punishment.

• Spending as much time with your Chow Chow as possible, even if it means simply keeping the dog in the room with you while you cook dinner or pay bills.

Common Mistakes to Avoid

Never pick your Chow Chow puppy up if they are showing fear or aggression toward an object, another dog, or person, because this will be rewarding them for unbalanced behavior.

If they are doing something you do not want them to continue, your puppy needs to be gently corrected by you with firm and calm energy, so that they learn not to react with fear or aggression. When the mum of the litter tells her puppies off, she will use a deep noise with strong eye contact, until the puppy quickly realizes it's doing something naughty.

Don't play the "hand" game, where you slide the puppy across the floor with your hands, because it's amusing for humans to see a little ball of fur scrambling to collect themselves and run back across the floor for another go.

This sort of "game" will teach your puppy to disrespect you as their leader in two different ways — first, because this "game" teaches them that humans are their play toys, and secondly, this type of "game" teaches them that humans are a source of excitement.

When your Chow Chow puppy is teething, they will naturally want to chew on everything within reach, and this will include you. As cute as you might think it is when they are young puppies, this is not an acceptable behavior, and you need to gently, but firmly, discourage the habit, just like a mother dog does to her puppies when they need to be weaned.

Always praise your puppy when they stop inappropriate behavior, as this is the beginning of teaching them to understand rules and boundaries. Often we humans are quick to discipline a puppy or dog for inappropriate behavior, but we forget to praise them for their good behavior.

Don't treat your Chow Chow like a small, furry human. When people try to turn dogs into people, this can cause them much stress and confusion that could lead to behavioral problems.

A well-behaved Chow Chow thrives on rules and boundaries, and when they understand that there is no question you are their leader and they are your follower, they will live a contented, happy and stress-free life.

Dogs are a different species with different rules; for example, they do not naturally cuddle, and they need to learn to be stroked and cuddled by humans. Therefore, be careful when approaching a dog for the first time and being overly expressive with your hands. The safest areas to touch are the back and chest — avoid patting on the head and touching the ears.

Many people will assume that a dog that is yawning is tired — this is often a misinterpretation, and instead it is signaling your dog is uncomfortable and nervous about a situation.

Be careful when staring at dogs because this is one of the ways in which they threaten each other. This body language can make them feel distinctly uneasy.

Habituation and Socialization

Habituation is when you continuously provide exposure to the same stimuli over a period of time. This will help your Chow Chow to relax in his environment and will teach him how to behave around unfamiliar people, noises, other pets, and different surroundings. Expose your Chow Chow puppy continuously to new sounds and new environments.

When you allow for your Chow Chow to face life's positive experiences through socialization and habituation, you're helping your Chow Chow to build a library of valuable information that he can use when he's faced with a difficult situation. If he's had plenty of wonderful and positive early experiences, the more likely he'll be able to bounce back from any surprising or scary experiences.

When your Chow Chow puppy arrives at his new home for the first time, he'll start bonding with his human family immediately. This will be his primary bond. His secondary bond will be with everyone outside your home. A dog should never be secluded inside his home. Be sure to find the right balance where you're not exposing your Chow Chow puppy to too much external stimuli. If he starts becoming fearful, speak to your veterinarian.

The puppyhood journey can be tiresome yet very rewarding. Primary socialization starts between three and five weeks of age, when a pup's experiences take place within his litter. This will have a huge impact on all his future emotional behavior.

Socialization from six to twelve weeks allows for puppies to bond with other species outside of their littermates and parents. It's at this particular stage that most pet parents will bring home a puppy and where he'll soon become comfortable with humans, other pets, and children.

By the time a puppy is around twelve to fourteen weeks, he becomes more difficult to introduce to new environments and new people and starts showing suspicion and distress.

Nonetheless, if you've recently adopted a Chow Chow puppy or are bringing one home and he's beyond this ideal age, don't neglect to continue the socialization process. Puppies need to be exposed to as many new situations, environments, people, and other animals as possible, and it is never too late to start.

During puppyhood, you can easily teach your puppy to politely greet a new person, yet by the time a puppy has reached social maturity, the same puppy, if not properly socialized, may start lunging forward and acting aggressively, with the final outcome of lunging and nipping.

Photo Credit: Vancie Drew of Mei-Ling Chow Chows

Never accidentally reward your Chow Chow puppy for displaying fear or growling at another dog or animal by picking them up. Picking up a Chow Chow puppy or dog at this time, when they are displaying unbalanced energy, actually turns out to be a reward for them, and you will be teaching them to continue with this type of behavior. As well, picking up a puppy literally places them in a "top dog" position where they are higher and more dominant than the dog or animal they just growled at.

The correct action to take in such a situation is to gently correct your puppy with a firm yet calm energy by distracting them with a "No," so that they learn to let you deal with the situation on their behalf.

If you allow a fearful or nervous puppy to deal with situations that unnerve them all by themselves, they may learn to react with fear or aggression, and you will have created a problem that could escalate into something quite serious as they grow older.

The same is true of situations where a young puppy may feel the need to protect themselves from a bigger or older dog that may come charging in for a sniff. It is the guardian's responsibility to protect the puppy so that they do not think they must react with fear or aggression in order to protect themselves.

Once your Chow Chow puppy has received all their vaccinations, you can take them out to public dog parks and various locations where many dogs are found.

Before allowing them to interact with other dogs or puppies, take them for a disciplined walk on leash so that they will be a little tired and less likely to immediately engage with all other dogs.

Keep your puppy on leash and close beside you, because most puppies are usually a bundle of out-of-control energy, and you need to protect them while teaching them how far they can go before getting themselves into trouble with adult dogs who may not appreciate excited puppy playfulness.

If your puppy shows any signs of aggression or domination toward another dog, you must immediately step in and calmly discipline them.

Take your puppy everywhere with you and introduce them to many different people of all ages, sizes, and ethnicities. Most people will come to you and want to interact with your puppy. If they ask if they can hold your puppy, let them, because so long as they are gentle and don't drop the puppy, this is a good way to socialize your Chow Chow and show them that humans are friendly.

As important as socialization is, it is also important that the dog be left alone for short periods when young so that they can cope with some periods of isolation. If an owner goes out and they have never experienced this, they can destroy things or make a mess because of panic. They are thinking they are vulnerable and can be attacked by something or someone coming into the house.

Dogs that have been socialized are able to easily diffuse a potentially troublesome situation and hence they will rarely get into fights. Dogs that are poorly socialized often misinterpret or do not understand the subtle signals of other dogs, getting into trouble as a result.

Creating a Safe Environment

Never think for a minute that your Chow Chow would not bolt and run away. Even well-adjusted, happy puppies and adult dogs can run away, usually in extreme conditions such as with fireworks, thunder, or when scared.

Collar, tag, and microchip your new Chow Chow. Microchipping is not enough, since many pet parents tend to presume that dogs without collars are homeless or have been abandoned. Recent photos of your Chow Chow with the latest clip need to be placed in your wallet or purse.

Train your Chow Chow – foster and work with a professional, positive trainer to ensure that your dog does not run out the front door or out the backyard gate. Teach your Chow Chow basic, simple commands such as "come" and "stay."

Create a special, fun digging area just for him, hide his bones and toys, and let your Chow Chow know that it's okay to dig in that area. After all, dogs need to play!

Introduce your new, furry companion to all your neighbors so everyone will know that he belongs to you.

Puppy Food and Nutrition

As Chows age, they thrive on a graduated program of nutrition. At age four months and younger, puppies should get four small meals a day. From age 4-8 months, three meals per day are appropriate. From 8 months on, feed your pet twice a day.

Be cautious about "free feeding" with any breed. Chows are not typically over-eaters, but scheduled feedings with measured amounts is the best nutritional approach for all dogs.

Begin feeding your puppy by putting the food down for 10-20 minutes. If the dog doesn't eat, or only eats part of the serving, still take the bowl up. Don't give the dog more until the next scheduled feeding.

To give your puppy a good start in life, rely on high quality, premium dry puppy food. If possible, replicate the puppy's existing diet. A sudden dietary switch can cause gastrointestinal upset. Maintain the dog's existing routine if practical.

To make an effective food transition, mix the existing diet with the new food, slowly changing the percentage of new to old over a period of 10 days.

The vast majority of breeders recommend not feeding puppy food. It can be high in protein and actually can cause the puppy to grow too fast, thus possibly creating bone growth issues.

Before buying any dog food, read the label. The first listed ingredients should be meat, fishmeal, or whole grains. Foods with large amounts of fillers like cornmeal or meat by-products have a low nutritional value. They fill your dog up, but don't give him the needed range of vitamins and minerals, and they increase daily waste produced.

Grain free (or raw) is often recommended for the Chow Chow. Many are allergic to corn, wheat, and some other grains. In addition, no "soy" should be in the dog food – it irritates them!

Wet foods are not appropriate for most growing dogs. They do not offer a good nutritional balance, and they are often upsetting to the stomach. Additionally, it's much harder to control portions with wet food, leading to young dogs being over or under fed.

Controlling portions is important. Give your dog the amount stipulated on the food packaging for his weight and age, and nothing more.

Invest in weighted food and water bowls made out of

stainless steel. The weights prevent the mess of "tip overs," and the material is much easier to clean than plastic. It does not hold odors or harbor bacteria.

Bowls in a stand that create an elevated feeding surface are also a good idea. Make sure your young dog can reach the food and water. Stainless steel bowl sets retail for less than $25 / £14.87.

A new water bowl that is great for Chows is called a hole bowl. Chows tend to wet their entire front when drinking, and the constant wet environment can lead to acute moist dermatitis (also called hot spots). The hole bowl lets them drink without drenching themselves.

Wendy Nieminen and Pete Dingwell of Bearcrest Chows advise: "Chows typically don't really have big appetites as adults. If they gobble at first it is just because they are used to competition from the littermates and will stop once they realize no one is trying to get their food. Later on when they get spayed or neutered, sometimes they have more of a tendency to gain weight, so you may then have to watch how much you feed.

"A spoon of plain yogurt or kefir is good for them as an add-in, but don't add in a lot of extras because that just throws a balanced dog food out of balance. They are getting the low protein requirements from the food so by adding in extra things like an egg or extra meat or cheese, you are now hiking the protein level up in their diet, and that is what we don't want.

"Reading labels on treat boxes is just as important because most of them are full of unhealthy ingredients. With these treats, you are adding the exact ingredients and chemicals you are trying to avoid back in their diets!"

Adult Nutrition

The same basic nutritional guidelines apply to adult Chow Chows. Always start with a high-quality, premium food. If possible, stay in the same product line the puppy received at the breeder. Graduated product lines help owners to create feeding programs that ensure nutritional consistency.

This approach allows you to transition your Chow away from puppy food to an adult mixture, and in time to a senior formula. This removes the guesswork from nutritional management.

Say No to Table Scraps!

Dogs don't make it easy to say no when they beg at the table. If you let a puppy have so much as that first bite, you run the risk of creating a little monster – and one with an unhealthy habit.

(Even acceptable treats formulated for dogs should never comprise more than 5% of a dog's daily food intake.)

Table scraps contributes to weight problems, and many human foods are toxic to dogs. Dangerous items include, but are not limited to:

- Chocolate
- Raisins
- Alcohol
- Human vitamins (especially those with iron)
- Mushrooms
- Onions and garlic
- Walnuts
- Macadamia nuts
- Raw fish
- Raw pork
- Raw chicken

If you give your puppy a bone, watch him. Use only bones that are too large to choke on and take the item away at the first sign of splintering. Commercial chew toys rated "puppy safe" are a much better option.

The Canine Teeth and Jaw

Even today, far too many dog food choices continue to have far more to do with being convenient for us humans to serve than they do with being a well-balanced, healthy food choice.

In order to choose the right food for your Chow Chow, first it's important to understand a little bit about canine physiology and what Mother Nature intended when she created our furry companions. While humans are omnivores who can derive energy from eating plants, our canine companions are natural carnivores, which means they derive their energy and nutrient requirements from eating a diet consisting mainly or exclusively of the flesh of animals, birds, or fish.

Although dogs can survive on an omnivorous diet, this does not mean it is the best diet for them. Unlike humans, who are equipped with wide, flat molars for grinding grains, vegetables, and other plant-based materials, canine teeth are all pointed because they are designed to rip, shred, and tear into meat and bone.

Another obvious consideration when choosing an appropriate food source for our furry friends is the fact that every canine is born equipped with powerful jaws and neck muscles for the specific purpose of being able to pull down and tear apart their hunted prey.

The structure of the jaw of every canine is such that it opens widely to hold large pieces of meat and bone, while the mechanics of a dog's jaw permits only vertical (up and down) movement that is designed for crushing.

The Canine Digestive Tract

A dog's digestive tract is short and simple and designed to move their natural choice of food (hide, meat, and bone) quickly through their systems.

The canine digestive system is simply unable to properly break down vegetable matter, which is why whole vegetables look pretty much the same going into your dog as they do coming out the other end.

Given the choice, most dogs would never choose to eat plants and grains, or vegetables and fruits over meat, however, we humans continue to feed them a kibble-based diet that contains high amounts of vegetables, fruits, and grains with low amounts of meat.

Part of this is because we've been taught that it's a healthy, balanced diet for humans, and therefore, we believe that it must be the same for our dogs, and part of this is because all the fillers that make up our dog's food are less expensive and easier to process than meat.

How much healthier and long lived might our beloved Chow Chow be if, instead of largely ignoring nature's design for our canine companions, we chose to feed them whole, unprocessed, species-appropriate food with the main ingredient being meat?

Whatever you decide to feed your dog, keep in mind that just as too much wheat, other grains, and fillers in our human diet is having a detrimental effect on our health, the same can be very true for our best fur friends.

Our dogs are also suffering from many of the same life-threatening diseases that are rampant in our human society as a direct result of consuming a diet high in genetically altered, impure, processed, and packaged foods.

The BARF Diet

Raw feeding advocates believe that the ideal diet for their dog is one that would be very similar to what a dog living in the wild would have access to, and these canine guardians are often opposed to feeding their dog any sort of commercially manufactured pet foods.

On the other hand, those opposed to feeding their dogs a raw or Biologically Appropriate Raw Food (BARF) diet believe that the risks associated with food-borne illnesses during the handling and feeding of raw meats outweigh the purported benefits.

Raw meats purchased at your local grocery store contain a much higher level of acceptable bacteria than raw food produced for dogs, because the meat purchased for human consumption is meant to be cooked, which will kill any bacteria.

This means that canine guardians feeding their dogs a raw food diet can be quite certain that commercially prepared raw foods sold in pet stores will be safer than raw meats purchased in grocery stores.

Many guardians of high-energy, working breed dogs will agree that their dogs thrive on a raw or BARF diet and strongly believe that the potential benefits of feeding a dog a raw food diet are many, including:

- Healthy, shiny coats
- Decreased shedding
- Fewer allergy problems
- Healthier skin
- Cleaner teeth
- Fresher breath
- Higher energy levels
- Improved digestion
- Smaller stools
- Strengthened immune system
- Increased mobility in arthritic pets
- General increase or improvement in overall health

All dogs, whether working breed or lap dogs, are amazing athletes in their own right, therefore every dog deserves to be fed the best food available.

A raw diet is a direct evolution of what dogs ate before they became our domesticated pets and we turned toward commercially prepared, easy-to-serve dry dog food that required no special storage or preparation.

The Dehydrated Diet

Dehydrated dog food comes in both raw and cooked forms, and these foods are usually air-dried to reduce moisture to the level where bacterial growth is inhibited.

The appearance of dehydrated dog food is very similar to dry kibble, and the typical feeding methods include adding warm water before serving, which makes this type of diet both healthy for our dogs and convenient for us to serve.

Dehydrated recipes are made from minimally processed fresh whole foods to create a healthy and nutritionally balanced meal that will meet or exceed the dietary requirements for healthy canines.

Dehydrating removes only the moisture from the fresh ingredients, which usually means that because the food has not already been cooked at a high temperature, more of the overall nutrition is retained.

A dehydrated diet is a convenient way to feed your dog a nutritious diet, because all you have to do is add warm water and wait five minutes while the food re-hydrates so your Chow Chow can enjoy a warm meal.

The Kibble Diet

While many canine guardians are starting to take a closer look at the food choices they are making for their furry companions, there is no mistaking that the convenience and relative economy of dry dog food kibble, which had its beginnings in the 1940s, continues to be the most popular pet food choice for most humans.

While feeding a high-quality, bagged kibble diet that has been flavored to appeal to dogs and supplemented with vegetables and fruits to appeal to humans may keep most every Chow Chow companion happy and healthy, you will need to decide whether this is the best diet for them.

Your Puppy's First Lessons

Don't give a young dog full run of the house before the puppy is house trained. Keep your new pet confined to a designated area behind a baby gate. This protects your home and possessions and keeps the dog safe from hazards like staircases. Depending on the size and configuration, baby gates retail from $25-$100 / £14.87-£59.46. During those times when you are not home to supervise the puppy, crate your pet.

Housebreaking

Crate training and housebreaking go hand in hand. Chows, like all dogs, come to see their crate as their den. They will hold their need to urinate or defecate while they are inside. Any time you leave the house, you should crate your pet, immediately taking the dog out upon your return.

Establishing and maintaining a daily routine also helps your dog in this respect. Feed your pet at the same time each day, taking him out afterwards. The feeding schedule dictates the frequency of "relief" breaks. Trips "out" will also decrease as the dog ages.

Don't be rigid in holding your puppy to this standard. Puppies have less control over their bladder and bowel movements than adult dogs. They need to go out more often, especially after they've been active or gotten excited.

On average, adult dogs go out 3-4 times a day: when they wake up, within an hour of eating, and right before bedtime. With puppies, don't wait more than 15 minutes after a meal.

Praise your pet with the same phrases to encourage and reinforce good elimination habits. NEVER punish a dog for having an accident. There is no association in the dog's mind with the punishment and the incident. Chows do respond to verbal scolding and they quickly learn not to do their "business" in the house. In fact, the breed is one of the easiest to house train.

If you catch your dog in the act of eliminating in the house, say "bad dog" in a stern, firm voice, but do not belabor the point. Your Chow will get the message. Clean up the accident using an enzymatic cleaner to eradicate the odor and return to the dog's normal routine. Nature's Miracle Stain and Odor Removal is an excellent product and is affordable at $5 / £2.97 per 32 ounce / 0.9 liter bottle.

The following are methods that you may or may not have considered, all of which have their own merits, including:

- Bell training
- Exercise pen training
- Free training
- Kennel training

All of these are effective methods, so long as you add in the one critical and often missing "wild card" ingredient, which is "human training."

When you bring home your new Chow Chow puppy, they will be relying upon your guidance to teach them what they need to learn, and when it comes to housetraining, the first thing the human guardian needs to learn is that the puppy is not being bad when they pee or poop inside.

They are just responding to the call of Mother Nature, and you need to pay close attention right from the very beginning, because it's entirely possible to teach a puppy to go to the bathroom outside in less than a week. Therefore, if your puppy is making bathroom "mistakes," blame yourself, not your puppy.

Check in with yourself and make sure your energy remains consistently calm and patient and that you exercise plenty of compassion and understanding while you help your new puppy learn the bathroom rules. Don't clean up after your puppy with them watching, as this makes the puppy believe you are there to clean up after them, making you lower in the dog pack order. While your puppy is still growing, on average, they can hold it approximately one hour for every month of their age. This means that if your 3-month-old puppy has been happily snoozing for two to three hours, as soon as they wake up, they will need to go outside.

Some of the first indications or signs that your puppy needs to be taken outside to relieve themselves will be when you see them:

• sniffing around
• circling
• looking for the door
• whining, crying, or barking
• acting agitated

During the early stages of potty training, adding treats as an extra incentive can be a good way to reinforce how happy you are that your puppy is learning to relieve themselves in the right place. Slowly, treats can be removed and replaced with your happy praise, or you can give your puppy a treat after they are back inside.

Next, now that you have a new puppy in your life, you will want to be flexible with respect to adapting your schedule to meet their internal clocks to quickly teach your Chow Chow puppy their new bathroom routine.

This means not leaving your puppy alone for endless hours at a time, because firstly, they are pack animals that need companionship and your direction at all times, plus long periods alone will result in the disruption of the potty training schedule you have worked hard to establish.

If you have no choice but to leave your puppy alone for many hours, make sure that you place them in a paper-lined room or pen where they can relieve themselves without destroying your newly installed hardwood or favorite carpet.

Remember, your Chow Chow is a growing puppy with a bladder and bowels that they do not yet have complete control over.

Bell Training

A very easy way to introduce your new Chow Chow puppy to house training is to begin by teaching them how to ring a doorbell whenever they need to go outside. A further benefit of training your puppy to ring a bell is that you will not have to listen to your puppy or dog whining, barking, or howling to be let out, and your door will not become scratched up from their nails.

Attach the bell to a piece of ribbon or string and hang it from a door handle or tape it to a doorsill near the door where you will be taking your puppy out when they need to relieve themselves. The string will need to be long enough so that your puppy can easily reach the bell with their nose or a paw.

Next, each time you take your puppy out to relieve themselves, say the word "out," and use their paw or their nose to ring the bell. Praise them for this "trick" and immediately take them outside. This type of an alert system is an easy way to eliminate accidents in the home.

Kennel Training

When you train your Chow Chow puppy to accept sleeping in their own kennel at nighttime, this will also help to accelerate their potty training. Because no puppy or dog wants to relieve themselves where they sleep, they will hold their bladder and bowels as long as they possibly can.
Presenting them with familiar scents by taking them to the same

spot in the yard or the same street corner will help to remind and encourage them that they are outside to relieve themselves. Use a voice cue to remind your puppy why they are outside, such as "go pee," and always remember to praise them every time they relieve themselves in the right place, so that they quickly understand what you expect of them.

Exercise Pen Training

The exercise pen is a transition from kennel-only training and will be helpful for those times when you may have to leave your Chow Chow puppy for more hours than they can reasonably be expected to hold it.

Exercise pens are usually constructed of wire sections that you can put together in whatever shape you desire, and the pen needs to be large enough to hold your puppy's kennel in one half of the pen, while the other half will be lined with newspapers or pee pads.

Place your Chow Chow puppy's food and water dishes next to the kennel and leave the kennel door open (or take it off), so they can wander in and out whenever they wish to eat or drink or go to the papers or pee pads if they need to relieve themselves.

Because they are already used to sleeping inside their kennel, they will not want to relieve themselves inside the area where they sleep. Therefore, your puppy will naturally go to the other half of the pen to relieve themselves on the newspapers or pee pads.

Free Training

If you would rather not confine your young Chow Chow puppy to one or two rooms in your home and will be allowing them to freely range about your home anywhere they wish during the day, this is considered free training.

Never get upset or scold a puppy for having an accident inside the home, because this will result in teaching your puppy to be afraid of you and to only relieve themselves in secret places or when you're not watching.

If you catch your Chow Chow puppy making a mistake, all that is necessary is for you to calmly say "no," quickly scoop them up, and take them outside or to their indoor bathroom area.

The Chow Chow is not a difficult puppy to housebreak, and they will generally do very well when you start them off with "puppy pee pads" that you will move closer and closer to the same door that you always use when taking them outside. This way, they will quickly learn to associate going to this door with when they need to relieve themselves.

Marking Territory

Both male and female dogs with intact reproductive systems mark territory by urinating. This is most often an outdoor behavior, but can happen inside if the dog is upset.

Again, use an enzymatic cleaner to remove the odor and minimize the attractiveness of the location to the dog. Territory marking is especially prevalent in intact males. The obvious long-term solution is to have the dog neutered.

Marking territory is not a consequence of poor house training. The behavior can be seen in dogs that would otherwise never "go" in the house. It stems from completely different urges and reactions.

Dealing with Separation Anxiety

Separation anxiety manifests in a variety of ways, ranging from vocalizations to nervous chewing. Dogs that are otherwise well trained may urinate or defecate in the house.

These behaviors begin when your dog recognizes signs that you are leaving. Triggers include picking up a set of car keys or putting on a coat. The dog may start to follow you around the house trying to get your attention, jumping up on you or otherwise trying to touch you.

It is imperative that you understand when you adopt a Chow that they are companion dogs. They must have time to connect and be with their humans. You are the center of your dog's world. The behavior that a dog exhibits when it has separation anxiety is not a case of the animal being "bad." The poor thing experiences real distress and loneliness.

The purpose of crate training is not to punish or imprison a dog. It is not a cruel or repressive measure. The crate is the dog's "safe place" and is a great coping mechanism for breeds with separation anxiety issues. You are not being mean or cruel teaching your dog to stay in a crate when you are away; you are *helping* your pet to cope.

Grooming

Do not allow yourself to get caught in the "my Chow doesn't like it" trap, which is an excuse many owners will use to avoid regular grooming sessions. When you allow your dog to dictate whether they will permit a grooming session, you are setting a dangerous precedent. Once you have bonded with your dog, they love to be tickled, rubbed, and scratched in certain favorite places. This is why grooming is a great source of pleasure and a way to bond.

The amount of grooming your Chow requires will depend on the length of his coat. They are clean dogs by nature and like to look their best. For this reason, Chows are agreeable about the whole process, but the sooner you start a grooming routine the better.

The Chow coat doesn't need to be trimmed, but regular brushing and bathing are a must. The recommendation is one bath per month minimum, with a good brushing at least once per week.

Wendy Nieminen and Pete Dingwell of Bearcrest Chows add: "Chows don't blow their puppy coat for quite a while, usually for the first year or so, but when it is time Mother Nature will definitely let you know it. It just falls out in clumps, but don't try to force it or let a groomer tell you otherwise. They have an undercoat and it is supposed to be there all year. In summer it keeps their skin cool and in winter keeps them warm. They do shed some of it twice a year as adults, but are always growing another. Never have them shaved! This will not keep them cool! It will have the opposite effect and expose their delicate skin to the sun and elements."

You will need a combination of brushes:

- Bristle brushes, which work well with all coats from long to short. They remove dirt and debris and distribute natural oils throughout the coat.

- Wire-pin brushes, which are for medium to long coats and look like a series of pins stuck in a raised base.

- Slicker brushes are excellent for smoothing and

detangling longer hair.

(Note: you can often find combination, two-headed brushes. They'll save you a little money and make your grooming sessions easier.)

Each of these types of brush costs less than $15 / £9 and often less than $10 / £6.

You may want to mist your pet first with a "coat dressing" product, which will control static and help to highlight the color and texture of the coat.

Brush on each side of the dog's body, using a slicker brush on areas of shorter hair and a wire-pin brush on the longer sections like the neck ruff. Finish off with a medium to coarse comb and a fine-toothed comb on the legs, feet, and face.

Be sure to brush all the way to the skin. Cut back any long, wispy hairs with shears and keep the area around the anus trimmed for sanitary purposes. Trimming may also be necessary on the hocks and at the ankles.

Grooming/brushing sessions are an excellent opportunity to examine your dog's skin. Look for any growths, lumps, bumps, or wounds. Additionally, have a good look at his ears, eyes, and mouth. Vigilant prevention is the hallmark of good healthcare for all companion animals. Watch for any discharge from the eyes or ears, as well accumulated debris in the ear canal and a foul or yeasty odor. (This is a sign of parasitical mite activity.)

Bathing

Most Chows are perfectly happy to have baths, and even seem

to enjoy the water. If, however, the process of giving your dog a bath daunts you, find a professional groomer who has experience with the breed. Most groomers are quite reasonable, charging in a range of $25-$50 / £15-£30 per session.

For "do it yourself" bathing, just remember not to get your pet's head and ears wet. Clean the dog's head and face with a warm, wet washcloth only. Rinse your dog's coat with clean, fresh water to remove all residues.

The rinse is really the most important step of the whole procedure. If any shampoo is left in the coat, it will irritate the skin and lead to "hot spots." Rinse the water through your pet's coat until it runs clear and then rinse again for good measure. Towel your pet dry and make sure he doesn't get chilled.

Nail Trimming

Coat maintenance is not the only grooming chore necessary to keep your Chow in good shape. Even dogs that walk on asphalt or other rough surfaces often will need to have their nails trimmed from time to time.

If your pet is agreeable, this is a job you can perform at home with a trimmer especially designed for use with dogs. I prefer those with plier grips. They're easier to handle and quite cost effective, selling for under $20 / £11.88.

Even better than a nail clipper is the electric Dremel tool because there is less chance of cutting into the quick. In addition, your dog's nails will be smooth, without the sharp edges clipping alone can create.

NOTE: never use a regular Dremel™ tool, as it will be too high speed and will burn your dog's toenails. Only use a slow speed Dremel™, such as Model 7300-PT Pet Nail Grooming Tool (approx. $40/£20). You can also purchase the flexible hose attachment for the Dremel which is much easier to handle and can be held like a pencil.

Snip off the nail tips at a 45-degree angle, being careful not to cut too far down. If you do, you'll catch the vascular quick, which will hurt the dog and cause heavy bleeding. If you are apprehensive about performing this chore, ask your vet tech or groomer to walk you through it the first time.

Photo Credit: Pam Godber of Lechan Chows

Anal Glands

All dogs can suffer from blocked anal glands. The dog may scoot or rub its bottom on the ground or carpet. (You may also notice a foul odor.)

If this occurs, the glands will need expressing to prevent an abscess from forming. This is a sensitive task and one that a veterinarian or an experienced groomer should perform.

Fleas And Ticks

I'm including fleas and ticks under grooming because that's when they're usually found. Don't think that if your Chow has "passengers" you're doing something wrong, or that the dog is at fault. This is a part of dog ownership. Sooner or later, it will happen. Address the problem, but don't "freak out."

Do NOT use a commercial flea product on a puppy of less than 12 weeks of age, and be extremely careful with adult dogs. Most of the major products contain pyrethrum. The chemical causes long-term neurological damage and even fatalities in small dogs.

To get rid of fleas, bathe your dog in warm water with a standard canine shampoo. Comb the animal's fur with a fine-toothed flea comb, which will trap the live parasites. Submerge the comb in hot soapy water to kill the fleas.

Wash the dog's bedding and any soft materials with which he has come in contact. Look for any accumulations of "flea dirt," which is blood excreted by adult fleas. Wash the bedding and other surfaces daily for at least a week to kill any remaining eggs before they hatch.

If you find a tick, coat it with a thick layer of petroleum jelly for 5 minutes to suffocate the parasite and cause its jaws to release. Pluck the tick off with a pair of tweezers using a straight motion.

Never just jerk a tick off a dog. The parasite's head stays behind and continues to burrow into the skin, making a painful sore.

Managing Your Chow's Activity

Chows have a low activity level and are suited for life in any home including an apartment. One or two brief walks per day will satisfy their exercise needs quite well.

Collar or Harness?

Regardless of breed, I'm not a big fan of using a traditional collar. I wouldn't enjoy a choking sensation and assume my dog wouldn't either. My current favorite on-body restraints are the harnesses that look like vests. They offer a point of attachment for the lead on the back between the shoulders.

This arrangement directs pressure away from the neck and allows for easy, free movement. Young dogs are less resistant to this system and don't strain against a harness the way they will with a collar.

It's best to take your dog with you to the pet store to get a proper fit. Sizing for a dog is much more unpredictable than you might think. I have seen dogs as large as 14 lbs. / 6.35 kg take an "Extra Small" depending on their build.

Regardless of size, harnesses retail in a range of $20 - $25 / £11.88 - £14.85.

Standard Leash or Retractable?

The decision to buy a standard, fixed-length leash or a retractable lead is, for the most part, a matter of personal preference. Some facilities like groomers, vet clinics, and dog daycares ask that you not use a retractable lead on their premises. The long line represents a trip and fall hazard for other human clients.

Fixed-length leashes often sell for as little as $5 / £2.97, while retractable leads are less than $15 / £8.91.

Learning to respond to your control of the leash is an important behavioral lesson for your Chow. Do not drag a dog on a lead or jerk him. If your young pet sits down and refuses to budge, pick him up. Don't let the dog be in charge of the walk, or you'll have the devil's own time regaining the upper hand.

Chows are smart dogs that love to be in the company of their humans. They'll associate the lead with that companionship and time with you. Don't be at all surprised if your dog picks up words associated with excursions like go, out, car, drive, or walk and responds accordingly.

Dog Walking Tips

Teach your dog to "sit" by using the word and making a downward pointing motion with your finger or indicating the desired direction with the palm of your hand. Do not attach the lead until your dog complies.

If your puppy jerks or pulls on the leash, stop, pick up the dog, and start the walk over with the "sit" command. Make it clear that the walk ceases when the dog misbehaves.

Praise your dog for walking well on the end of the lead and for stopping when you stop. Reinforce positive behaviors during walks. Your dog will get the message and show the same traits during other activities.

The Importance of Basic Commands

It is to your advantage to go through a basic obedience class with your dog. Chows are not as eager to please as other dogs, but they are deeply bonded to their humans. They make excellent students, and respond well to a consistent routine and command "language."

Experts agree that most dogs can pick up between 165 and 200 words, but they can't extrapolate more than one meaning. If, for instance, your dog barks, you need to use the same "command" in response, like "quiet." If he picks something up, you might say "drop it."

For problem jumping, most owners go with "down." The point is to pick a set of words and use them over and over again to create a basic vocabulary for your dog. Both the word and your tone of voice should convey your authority and elicit the desired response.

This is not a difficult process with a breed whose native intelligence is as advanced as that of the Chow. Investigate enrollment in an obedience class through your local big box pet store, or ask your vet about trainers in your area. It is to your advantage if you can locate a trainer who has experience with the breed. Start the lessons early in your dog's life by offering him the stability of consistent reactions.

Play Time and Tricks

Do not mistake intelligence for trainability or responsiveness to training as an indication that your Chow will do tricks. They can learn anything, but if they don't see a purpose for the action, their native stubbornness kicks in and they won't do a thing.

You best option is to learn your own dog. Find out what your Chow likes to do and more or less ask him if he's willing to take the behavior to the level of a trick. He may look at you gravely like you've lost your mind, but he will at least be open to having the conversation.

If you do get a Chow to perform some sort of "trick," always offer praise and show pleasure in his behavior. He's only done the bit of foolery to please you, so be nice about it.

Chows are not big chewers, but all dogs need chew toys for better dental health. Don't select toys that are soft and "shredable." I recommend chew toys like Nylabones that can withstand the abuse. You can buy items made out of this tough material in the $1-$5 / £0.59-£2.97 range.

Never give your dog rawhide or pig's ears, which soften and present a choking hazard. In addition, avoid cow hooves, which can splinter and puncture the cheek or palate.

Photo Credit: Tammy Tosh of Hsot Chow Chows

Avoid soft rubber toys. They shred into small pieces, which the dog will swallow. Opt for rope toys instead. Don't buy anything with a squeaker or any other part that presents a choking hazard.

Playtime is important, especially for a dog's natural desire to chase. Try channeling this instinct with toys and games. If a dog has no stimulation and has nothing to chase, they can start to chase their own tail, which can lead to problems.

Toys can be used to simulate the dog's natural desire to hunt. For example, when they catch a toy, they will often shake it and bury their teeth into it, simulating the killing of their prey.

It should also be noted that many Chows still have hunting genes, which makes a fenced in yard a must.

Allow your dog to fulfill a natural desire to chew. This comes from historically catching their prey and then chewing the carcass. Providing chews or bones can prevent your dog from destroying your home.

Playing with your dog is not only a great way of getting them to use up their energy, but it is also a great way of bonding with them as they have fun. Dogs love to chase and catch balls, just make sure that the ball is too large to be swallowed.

Deer antlers are wonderful toys for a Chow Chow. Most love them. They do not smell, are all-natural, and do not stain or splinter. I recommend the antlers that are not split, as they last longer.

Dogs that don't get enough exercise are also more likely to develop problem behaviors like chewing, digging, and barking.

Chapter 6 - Training and Problem Behaviors

Chows are stubborn to the point of being pig headed. Any dog, regardless of breed, can exhibit poor behaviors. Chows are often possessive of both their owners and their territory, and they do not always do well with strangers, especially those that arrive unannounced and are not introduced to the dog by the Chow's human.

Photo Credit: Wendy Nieminen & Pete Dingwell of Bearcrest Chows

Negative behavior may not target humans. The dog may act out toward other dogs through snapping, lunging, pushing, barking, or baring of the teeth. Chows may be especially aggressive with dogs of equal size and of the same gender. Most of these potential problem behaviors can be overcome with proper socialization starting at a young age.

Take your puppy to a training class. Introduce him to new sights, sounds, people, and places. Let him interact with other dogs in a controlled environment. There, the dog is safe to deal with fear and timidity without blustering self-defense postures, but more importantly, he will learn to tailor his reaction to your own.

You'll get a better-mannered dog and a greater understanding of how to guide your pet's future interactions.

Responsible dog owners are attentive to the behavior of their own dog and to what's going on around them. They praise good behavior, but accept responsibility for anticipating potential clashes. Often in a public setting, the wisest course of action is to avoid a meeting with another dog altogether.

In the last chapter, I discussed leash training, which is crucial for successful public outings. Rather than avoiding areas with other people and dogs, your goal is to be able to take your dog to such places without incident. Contrary to what some people think, well-managed outings in varied environments help to create confidence in your dog.

I asked Tammy Tosh of Hsot Chow Chows if she thought Chows were more difficult to train compared to most other breeds:

"Chows are extremely intelligent. Having worked for a veterinarian for over 25 years, I have seen nearly every breed imaginable and I can tell you that a Chow will not do something unless he sees a reason that benefits him. A Labrador will chase a ball over and over, a Chow will do it once and then think this is just dumb, I see no reason to keep doing this, and will stop fetching it.

"Training them has to be done in a manner in which there is something in it for them. You have to stay one step ahead of them. In my opinion, they are probably THE smartest dogs, as they do not act like a dog at all. It's like training a cat, not so easy. If you can find what motivates them, they pick up on things very quickly."

Dog Whispering

Many people can be confused when they need professional help with their dog because for many years, if you needed help with your dog, you contacted a "dog trainer" or took your dog to "puppy classes," where your dog would learn how to sit or stay.

The difference between a dog trainer and a dog whisperer would be that a "dog trainer" teaches a dog how to perform certain tasks, and a "dog whisperer" alleviates behavior problems by teaching humans what they need to do to keep their particular dog happy.

Often, depending on how soon the guardian has sought help, this can mean that the dog in question has developed some pretty serious issues, such as aggressive barking, lunging, biting, or attacking other dogs, pets, or people.

Dog whispering is often an emotional roller coaster ride for the humans involved that unveils many truths when they finally realize that it has been their actions (or inactions) that have likely caused the unbalanced behavior that their dog is now displaying.

Once solutions are provided, the relief for both dog and human can be quite cathartic when they realize that with the correct direction, they can indeed live a happy life with their dog.

All specific methods of training, such as "clicker training," fall outside of what every dog needs to be happy, because training your dog to respond to a clicker, which you can easily do on your own, and then letting them sleep in your bed, eat from your plate, and any other multitude of things humans allow, are what makes the dog unbalanced and causes behavior problems.

I always say to people, don't wait until you have a severe problem before getting some dog whispering or professional help of some sort, because "With the proper training, Man can learn to be dog's best friend."

Rewarding Unwanted Behavior

It is very important to recognize that any attention paid to an out-of-control, adolescent puppy, even negative attention, is likely to be exciting and rewarding for your Chow Chow puppy.

Chasing after a puppy when they have taken something they shouldn't have, picking them up when barking or showing aggression, pushing them off when they jump on other people, or yelling when they refuse to come when called are all forms of attention that can actually be rewarding for most puppies.

It will be your responsibility to provide structure for your puppy, which will include finding acceptable and safe ways to allow your puppy to vent their energy without being destructive or harmful to others.

The worst thing you can do when training your Chow Chow is to yell at him or use punishment. Positive reinforcement training methods – that is, rewarding your dog for good behavior – are infinitely more effective than negative reinforcement – training by punishment.

It is important when training your Chow Chow that you do not allow yourself to get frustrated. If you feel yourself starting to get angry, take a break and come back to the training session later.

Why is punishment-based training so bad? Think about it this way – your dog should listen to you because he wants to please you, right?

If you train your dog using punishment, he could become fearful of you and that could put a damper on your relationship with him. Do your dog and yourself a favor by using positive reinforcement.

Teaching Basic Commands

When it comes to training your Chow Chow, you have to start off slowly with the basic commands. The most popular basic commands for dogs include sit, down, stay, and come.

Sit

This is the most basic and one of the most important commands you can teach your Chow Chow.

1.) Stand in front of your Chow Chow with a few small treats in your pocket.

2.) Hold one treat in your dominant hand and wave it in front of your Chow Chow's nose so he gets the scent.

3.) Give the "Sit" command.

4.) Move the treat upward and backward over your Chow Chow's head so he is forced to raise his head to follow it.

5.) In the process, his bottom will lower to the ground.

6.) As soon as your Chow Chow's bottom hits the ground, praise him and give him the treat.

7.)   Repeat this process several times until your dog gets the hang of it and responds consistently.

Photo Credit: Vancie Drew of Mei-Ling Chow Chows

Down

After the "Sit" command, "Down" is the next logical command to teach because it is a progression from "Sit."

1.)   Kneel in front of your Chow Chow with a few small treats in your pocket.

2.)   Hold one treat in your dominant hand and give your Chow Chow the "Sit" command.

3.)   Reward your Chow Chow for sitting, then give him the "Down" command.

4.)   Quickly move the treat down to the floor between your Chow Chow's paws.

5.)   Your dog will follow the treat and should lie down to retrieve it.

6.)   Praise and reward your Chow Chow when he lies down.

7.)   Repeat this process several times until your dog gets the hang of it and responds consistently.

Come

It is very important that your Chow Chow responds to a "Come" command, because there may come a time when you need to get his attention and call him to your side during a dangerous situation (such as him running around too close to traffic).

1.)   Put your Chow Chow on a short leash and stand in front of him.

2.)   Give your Chow Chow the "Come" command, then quickly take a few steps backward away from him.

3.)   Clap your hands and act excited, but do not repeat the "Come" command.

4.)   Keep moving backwards in small steps until your Chow Chow follows and comes to you.

5.)   Praise and reward your Chow Chow and repeat the process.

6.)   Over time, you can use a longer leash or take your Chow Chow off the leash entirely.

7.)   You can also start by standing further from your Chow Chow when you give the "Come" command.

8.)   If your Chow Chow doesn't come to you immediately, you can use the leash to pull him toward you.

Stay

This command is very important because it teaches your Chow Chow discipline – not only does it teach your Chow Chow to stay, but it also forces him to listen and pay attention to you.

1.)   Find a friend to help you with this training session.

2.)   Have your friend hold your Chow Chow on the leash while you stand in front of the dog.

3.)   Give your Chow Chow the "Sit" command and reward him for responding correctly.

4.)   Give your dog the "Stay" command while holding your hand out like a "Stop" sign.

5.)   Take a few steps backward away from your dog and pause for 1 to 2 seconds.

6.)   Step back toward your Chow Chow, then praise and reward your dog.

7.)   Repeat the process several times, then start moving back a little further before you return to your dog.

Beyond Basic Training

Once your Chow Chow has a firm grasp on the basics, you can move on to teaching him additional commands. You can also add distractions to the equation to reinforce your dog's mastery of the commands. The end goal is to ensure that your Chow

Chow responds to your command each and every time – regardless of distractions and anything else he might rather be doing. This is incredibly important, because there may come a time when your dog is in a dangerous situation and if he doesn't respond to your command, he could get hurt.

After your Chow Chow has started to respond correctly to the basic commands on a regular basis, you can start to incorporate distractions.

If you previously conducted your training sessions indoors, you might consider moving them outside where your dog could be distracted by various sights, smells, and sounds.

One thing you might try is to give your dog the Stay command and then toss a toy nearby that will tempt him to break his Stay. Start by tossing the toy at a good distance from him and wait a few seconds before you release him to play.

Eventually you will be able to toss a toy right next to your dog without him breaking his Stay until you give him permission to do so.

Incorporating Hand Signals

Teaching your Chow Chow to respond to hand signals in addition to verbal commands is very useful – you never know when you will be in a situation where your dog might not be able to hear you.

To start out, choose your dominant hand to give the hand signals, and hold a small treat in that hand while you are training your dog – this will encourage your dog to focus on your hand during training, and it will help to cement the connection between the command and the hand signal.

To begin, give your dog the Sit or Down command while holding the treat in your dominant hand and give the appropriate hand signal – for Sit you might try a closed fist and for Down, you might place your hand flat, parallel to the ground.

When your dog responds correctly, give him the treat. You will need to repeat this process many times in order for your dog to form a connection between both the verbal command and the hand signal with the desired behavior.

Eventually, you can start to remove the verbal command from the equation – use the hand gesture every time, but start to use the verbal command only half the time.

Once your dog gets the hang of this, you should start to remove the food reward from the equation. Continue to give your dog the hand signal for each command, and occasionally use the verbal command just to remind him.

You should start to phase out the food rewards, however, by offering them only half the time. Progressively lessen the use of the food reward, but continue to praise your dog for performing the behavior correctly so he learns to repeat it.

Teaching Distance Commands

In addition to getting your dog to respond to hand signals, it is also useful to teach him to respond to your commands even when you are not directly next to him.

This may come in handy if your dog is running around outside and gets too close to the street – you should be able to give him a Sit or Down command so he stops before he gets into a dangerous situation.

Teaching your dog distance commands is not difficult, but it does require some time and patience.

To start, give your Chow Chow a brief refresher course of the basic commands while you are standing or kneeling right next to him.

Next, give your dog the Sit and Stay commands, then move a few feet away before you give the Come command.

Repeat this process, increasing the distance between you and your dog before giving him the Come command. Be sure to praise and reward your dog for responding appropriately when he does so.

Once your dog gets the hang of coming on command from a distance, you can start to incorporate other commands.

One method of doing so is to teach your dog to sit when you grab his collar. To do so, let your dog wander freely and every once in a while walk up and grab his collar while giving the Sit command.

After a few repetitions, your dog should begin to respond with a Sit when you grab his collar, even if you do not give the command.

Gradually, you can increase the distance from which you come to grab his collar and give him the command.

After your dog starts to respond consistently when you come from a distance to grab his collar, you can start giving the Sit command without moving toward him.

It may take your dog a few times to get the hang of it, so be patient. If your dog doesn't Sit right away, calmly walk up to him and repeat the Sit command, but do not grab his collar this time.

Eventually, your dog will get the hang of it, and you can start to practice using other commands like Down and Stay from a distance.

Clicker Training

When it comes to training your Chow Chow, you are going to be most successful if you maintain consistency. Chow Chows have a tendency to be a little stubborn, so unless you are very clear with your dog about what your expectations are, he may simply decide not to follow your commands.

A simple way to achieve consistency in training your Chow Chow is to use the principles of clicker training. Clicker training involves using a small handheld device that makes a clicking noise when you press it between your fingers.

Clicker training is based on the theory of operant conditioning, which helps your dog to make the connection between the desired behavior and the offering of a reward.

Chow Chows have a natural desire to please, so if they learn that a certain behavior earns your approval, they will be eager to repeat it – clicker training is a great way to help your dog quickly identify the particular behavior you want him to repeat.

All you have to do is give your Chow Chow a command and, as soon as he performs the behavior, you use the clicker. After you use the clicker, give your dog the reward as you would with any form of positive reinforcement training.

Some of the benefits of clicker training include:

- Very easy to implement – all you need is the clicker.
- Helps your dog form a connection between the command and the desired behavior more quickly.
- You only need to use the clicker until your dog makes the connection, then you can stop.
- May help to keep your dog's attention more effectively if he hears the noise.

Clicker training is just one method of positive reinforcement training that you can consider for training your Chow Chow.

No matter what method you choose, it is important that you maintain consistency and always praise and reward your dog for responding to your commands correctly so he learns to repeat the behavior.

First Tricks

When teaching your Chow Chow their first tricks, in order to give them extra incentive, find a small treat that they would do anything to get, and give the treat as a reward to help solidify a good performance.

Most dogs will be extra attentive during training sessions when they know that they will be rewarded with their favorite treats.

If your Chow Chow is less than six months old when you begin teaching them tricks, keep your training sessions short (no more than 5 or 10 minutes) and make the sessions lots of fun.

As your Chow Chow becomes an adult, you can extend your sessions because they will be able to maintain their focus for longer periods of time.

Photo Credit: Bernice Leroy of Ciao Chows - Self-red smooth male pup of 7 months. Very dark mahogany red. Ciao Born of Fire – "Kenny"

Shake a Paw

Who doesn't love a dog who knows how to shake a paw? This is one of the easiest tricks to teach your Chow Chow.

Practice every day until they are 100% reliable with this trick, and then it will be time to add another trick to their repertoire.

Most dogs are naturally either right or left pawed. If you know which paw your dog favors, ask them to shake this paw.

Find a quiet place to practice, without noisy distractions or other pets, and stand or sit in front of your dog. Place them in the sitting position and hold a treat in your left hand.

Say the command "Shake" while putting your right hand behind their left or right paw and pulling the paw gently toward yourself until you are holding their paw in your hand. Immediately praise them and give them the treat.

Most dogs will learn the "Shake" trick very quickly, and in no time at all, once you put out your hand, your Chow Chow will immediately lift their paw and put it into your hand, without your assistance or any verbal cue.

Roll Over

You will find that just like your Chow Chow is naturally either right or left pawed, that they will also naturally want to roll to either the right or the left side.

Take advantage of this by asking your dog to roll to the side they naturally prefer. Sit with your dog on the floor and put them in a lie down position.

Hold a treat in your hand and place it close to their nose without allowing them to grab it, and while they are in the lying position, move the treat to the right or left side of their head so that they have to roll over to get to it.

You will quickly see which side they want to naturally roll to; once you see this, move the treat to that side. Once they roll over to that side, immediately give them the treat and praise them.

You can say the verbal cue "Over" while you demonstrate the hand signal motion (moving your right hand in a half circular motion) from one side of their head to the other.

Sit Pretty

While this trick is a little more complicated, and most dogs pick up on it very quickly, remember that this trick requires balance, and every dog is different, so always exercise patience.

Find a quiet space with few distractions and sit or stand in front of your dog and ask them to "Sit."

Have a treat nearby (on a countertop or table) and when they sit, use both of your hands to lift up their front paws into the sitting pretty position, while saying the command "Sit Pretty." Help them balance in this position while you praise them and give them the treat.

Once your Chow Chow can do the balancing part of the trick quite easily without your help, sit or stand in front of your dog while asking them to "Sit Pretty" and hold the treat above their head, at the level their nose would be when they sit pretty.

If they attempt to stand on their back legs to get the treat, you may be holding the treat too high, which will encourage them to stand up on their back legs to reach it. Go back to the first step and put them back into the "Sit" position, and again lift their paws while their backside remains on the floor.

The hand signal for "Sit Pretty" is a straight arm held over your dog's head with a closed fist. Place your Chow Chow beside a wall when first teaching this trick so that they can use the wall to help their balance.

A young Chow Chow puppy should be able to easily learn these basic tricks before they are six months old, and when you are patient and make your training sessions short and fun for your dog, they will be eager to learn more.

Excessive Jumping

Allowing any dog to jump is a serious mistake, although it does not tend to be a problem with this breed. However, jumping is one of the most undesirable of all traits and thus worthy of mention.

Many people are afraid of dogs, and find spontaneous jumping threatening. Don't make the mistake of assuming that excessive jumping is an expression of friendliness. All too often, it's a case of a dominant dog asserting his authority and saying, "I don't respect you."

Dogs that know their proper place in the "pack" don't jump on more dominant dogs. A jumper sees himself as the "top dog" in all situations.

As the dog's master, you must enforce the "no jumping" rule. Anything else will only confuse your pet. Dogs have a keen perception of space. Rather than retreating from a jumping dog, step sideways and forward, taking back your space that he is trying to claim.

You are not trying to knock your dog down, but he may careen into you and fall anyway. Remain casual and calm. Take slow, deliberate motions and protect the "bubble" around your body. Your dog won't be expecting this action from you, and won't enjoy it. After several failed jumps, the dog will lose interest when his dominant message is no longer getting across.

Barking Behavior

Chows are excellent watchdogs and will bark to alert their humans of a potential intruder, however, excessive barking creates serious problems, especially if you live near other people. If you are in an apartment complex with shared walls, a barking dog can get you thrown out of your home. To get to the bottom of problem barking, you must first try to figure out what is setting your dog off.

Is he lonely? bored? wanting attention? overly excited? anxious? Is he responding to something he's seeing? hearing? smelling?

As with all problem behaviors, address barking with patience and consistency. If a firm, "No" or "Quiet" fails to work, try spraying your dog with water from a mister or squirt gun. Aim for the face. You won't hurt your pet, but you will get his attention. (Do be careful about your pet's eyes.)

For real problem barkers, humane bark collars can teach the dog through negative reinforcement. These collars release a harmless spray of citronella into the dog's nose in response to vibrations in the throat. The system, though somewhat expensive at $100/£60, works in almost all cases.

Chewing

Again, Chows do not have a reputation for being problem chewers, but this is a natural behavior in dogs that should be discussed. If left undirected, a dog with a fetish for chewing is capable of causing unbelievable levels of destruction in your home. Excessive chewing indicates some combination of anxiety or boredom, which may mean you need to get your dog out of the house more.

Regardless, make sure your dog has proper chew toys, like Nylabones, that exist to be destroyed! If you catch your pet chewing on a forbidden object, reprimand him and take the item away. Immediately substitute an appropriate chew toy.

Digging

Digging is not a problem in Chows, but if it gets started, especially indoors, the behavior is an expression of fear, anxiety, and/or boredom.

Digging is a difficult behavior to stop. An out-of-control digger can destroy your sofa or some other piece of furniture. The best solution is to spend more time playing with and exercising your pet.

Moreover, consider enrolling your pet in a dog daycare facility so he will not be alone while you are at work and thus less susceptible to separation anxiety.

Photo Credit: Margit and Bernd Lassen of Chow Chow of Peking

Begging

Any dog will beg at the table if allowed to do so. My best advice to you is never to allow this behavior to get started. Make "people" food off limits from day one.

If your pet becomes a serious beggar, confine him to another part of the house during meal times. This is as a control measure for you and other people at the table. If you can't ignore the pointed, unblinking stare of a Chow determined to share your dinner, you're the real problem!

Chasing

Chows do have a strong hunting instinct, and they will chase smaller animals of all types.

When you are out with your dog, especially near busy urban areas, you must keep your pet leashed at all times. Never allow your dog off the leash unless you are in a fenced, completely secure area.

A Chow can easily become so intent on the chase, they will not come when called and do not pay attention to dangers in their immediate area, including cars – not to mention the potential of a tragic end for the small creature being chased.

Biting

Another Chow Chow myth is that they are problem biters, as Tiffany Maddux of RHR Chow Chows explains: "I find this quite the opposite. Even adult rescue Chows that have come to me from bad situations will not snap or bite unless they are pushed. If given the option they will leave the situation or turn away from you. They are a defensive breed not offensive, like say a German Shepherd."

Any dog will bite if he is reacting out of pain or fear. Biting is a primary means of defense. Use socialization, obedience training, and stern corrections to control a puppy's playful nips.

If an adult dog displays biting behavior, it is imperative to get to the bottom of the biting. Have the dog evaluated for a health problem and work with a professional trainer.

Chapter 7 - Interested in Showing Your Chow Chow?

If you have purchased a show-quality Chow Chow and are planning to enter the world of dog shows and the dog fancy, you have a whole education in front of you.

If you have not already done so, you will want to begin to attend dog shows and to make connections in the world of the dog fancy to acquire the training to participate with your Chow, or to hire someone to show the animal for you.

Photo Credit: MBISS GCH CH Dreamland's Startin' A Revolution......having fun winning the breed at Westminster 2014. Breeders/Owners: Michael & Linda Brantley, CO Owners: Kathy Sylvia & Doug Stewart

The best thing you can do if you are planning to show your puppy is socializing them once they have settled in their new home. The work you put in at this stage of your puppy's life will shape them for life, so you need to get it right, take it slowly, and build it up gently. Remember: they are only babies, and they need to know you are there for them and are in charge of every situation.

Your puppy needs to be happy for a judge to run their hands all over them, so it is very important to get them used to this. When your Chow Chow puppy is happy for you to be able to touch them all over, you can get your trusted friends to do the same. Start at the head, look in their ears and eyes, and run your hands all down their back and down their legs.

What Dogs Are Qualified to Participate?

For a dog to participate in a dog show, it must be registered with the governing body for that exhibition. For instance, dogs registered with the American Kennel Club that are 6 months or older on the day of the show are eligible to enter AKC sponsored events. Spayed or neutered dogs are not eligible, nor are dogs with disqualifying faults according to the accepted standard for the breed.

It's generally easier to show a male, as opposed to a female, because females can be hard on their coat and change behavior during their heat cycles.

Joining a Breed Club

When you attend a dog show, find out about joining a breed-specific club in your area. Such groups usually sponsor classes to teach the basics in handling and showing the breed or will have contacts to put you in touch with individual teachers.

Breed club membership is also important to learn the culture of the dog fancy and to meet people in the show world. You will begin by participating in smaller, local shows to learn the ropes before entering an event that will garner points toward sanctioned titles within a governing group's system.

There are also "fun matches" that a new dog owner can participate in open to dogs from 3-6 months of age. Here they can get an idea of how dog show judging takes place. It's also a great training ground for that future show prospect.

The more you know about your breed, its care and maintenance, and the handling of them, the better you will be in the show ring. Study your country's parent kennel club's official breed standard.

Hiring a Professional

It is not uncommon for people who own show quality animals to hire professional handlers to work with the dogs.

If you are interested in going this route, be sure to interview several handlers and to get a full schedule of their rates. Attend a show where they are working with a dog and watch them in action. Ask for references, and contact the people whose names you are given.

Entrusting a handler with the care of your dog is an enormous leap of faith. You want to be certain you have hired someone with whom you are completely comfortable and with whom your dog has an observable rapport.

Don't Be Put Off by Fear

My advice to folks who are interested in starting to show is go to several shows and watch the dogs in the ring. Talk to the folks at the sidelines; most are very happy to talk dogs with you.

Find a successful show person to evaluate the dog you plan to start showing. Although anybody can show a dog, you need to get an objective appraisal of your dog's qualities. To qualify as a show dog, it can't have any disqualifying faults, so it is important you find a mentor who can honestly help you evaluate your dog.

I also advise you to attend conformation classes in your area if possible, and be sure your dog is well socialized. Most local Kennel Clubs offer these classes at very reasonable rates. Presentation and the dog's attitude are also a very important factor. Shy and timid dogs usually don't do well at a dog show.

Photo Credit: Pam Godber of Lechan Chows

Don't forget that judges' assignments are to assess the breeding stock quality of the exhibits before them via the official breed standard description, observations on movement, and their hands-on experience. There are good judges and the opposite. Many owners have found that performance events, such as obedience, agility, rally, and therapy dog provide great satisfaction in lieu of conformation events.

Of course, you always hope your dog will win. If you have done all your homework, and your dog is a good representative of the breed, you should walk in the ring with confidence and present your dog as best as possible. There is no such thing as a perfect dog, and a good handler will know how to hide the faults and show off the best traits.

I always found going to a dog show exciting. You should always think of it as fun. It will give you an opportunity to meet many people who are also fanciers of your particular breed. Try to learn as much as possible. Hopefully, you will find people who are willing to help.

Although it is a competition, whether you win or lose, you should always be a good sport. Remember, there is always another show and another judge and different competition. After a while, you will get to know which judges like a particular type or style of your breed.

Show Tips and Advice

Make sure you are well organized. Get to the show at least an hour before you are in the ring, as this will give you and your dog time to settle down.

Make sure you have your ring number on when you enter the ring. Make a strong entrance – you only get one chance to make an impression. Remember, the judge will look across the ring from time to time, so have your dog facing the judge even when you are relaxed. Always keep an eye on the judge. Before you set off, have your arm in an L shape. It will help you keep in a straight line and have more control. Look at something in front of you, keep your eyes on it, and move towards it. Say your dog's name, then say move.

Never give treats when you are moving your dog, as your dog will look up at you, and you need them to go in a straight line. In addition, don't give treats when the judge is going over your dog. Save the treat your dog loves the most for shows, not training, so you can get their attention even more so.

Don't get boxed in a corner at the show; give yourself plenty of room by not standing too close to other exhibiters.

MBISS GCH CH Dreamland's American Revolution, Winning the National Specialty under breeder judge Paul Odenkirchen 2011. Breeders: Michael & Linda Brantley, handler: Linda Brantley

Always dress smart, wear good shoes you can run in, and if you're a woman, wear a sports bra.

Hold your head up, try to look confident, and look like a winner. The judge needs to know you can hold your own and show your dog off in the big ring. If you look too shy, they may think you are not up to the job of representing your breed in the group ring.

Always have a cloth to wipe your dog's mouth dry. Do this just before it's your turn to stand your dog for the judge. It makes showing the bite so much easier.

Warm your dog up before you go in the ring by having a little practice run.

Finally, always take your dog to show in good, clean condition.

The Westminster Dog Show and Crufts

So how does an owner get to take part in the famous Westminster Dog Show in the United States?

Well, it is a requirement that in order to compete, your dog must already be a champion. The entry forms are sent out in October of the previous year, and the limit is usually reached that same day. Dogs that have been exhibited the previous year will automatically get their entries accepted. It's pretty difficult for a novice or amateur handler to get their entries in on time.

To qualify for Crufts, you need to place at least 3rd in your class at a Championship show where Challenge certificates are on offer. Pam Godber of Lechan Chows adds, "Note that no trimming of a Chow coat is allowed in the UK (in the breed standard). We as UK exhibitors find this means that at shows with overseas exhibitors, it is not a level playing field."

Chapter 8 – Chow Chow Health

You are your Chow's primary healthcare provider. You will know what is "normal" for your dog. Yours will be the best sense that something is "wrong," even when there is no obvious injury or illness. The more you understand preventive health care, the better you will care for your dog throughout his life.

I asked Linda Fernandez of Cherub Chows what health issues new Chow Chow owners should be aware of:

"The breeders before me worked really hard on the health issues Chows had and they improved them greatly. Good breeders don't have a lot of health issues at this time because you have several generations of testing before you have the dog you have now. An ethical breeder gets basic tests done – hips, patellas, elbows, and eyes are tested.

"My Chows have fairly long lives that they enjoy until they are at least 14 quite trouble-free. They eat the same food and go outside and remain house trained, but they sleep so much more. Somewhere after 14 years, I notice a change. Ch. Cherub Killing

Me Softly (Primo) lived to be 16. He slept so soundly, I had a singleton puppy that was 3 weeks old that slept on his tail for his nap. Primo was black and the puppy was a cream. So much for fierce Chows!"

Your Veterinarian Is Your Partner

Working with a qualified veterinarian is critical to long-term and comprehensive healthcare. If you do not already have a vet, ask your breeder for a recommendation. If you purchased your pet outside your area, contact your local dog club and ask for referrals.

Make an appointment to tour the clinic and meet the vet. Be clear about the purpose of your visit and about your intent to pay the regular office fee. Don't expect to get a freebie interview, and don't waste anyone's time! Go in with a set of prepared questions:

- How long has this practice been in operation?
- How many vets are on staff?
- Are any of your doctors specialists?
- If not, to which doctors do you refer patients?
- What are your regular business hours?
- Do you recommend a specific emergency clinic?
- Do you have emergency hours?
- What specific medical services do you offer?
- Do you offer grooming services?
- May I have an estimated schedule of fees?
- Do you currently treat any Chow Chows?

Pay attention to all aspects of your visit, including how the facilities appear and the demeanor of the staff. Things to look for include:

- how the staff interacts with clients
- the degree of organization or lack thereof
- indications of engagement with the clientele (office bulletin board, cards, and photos displayed, etc.)
- quality of all visible equipment
- cleanliness and orderliness of the waiting area and back rooms
- prominent display of doctors' credentials

These are only some suggestions. Go with your "gut." If the clinic and staff seems to "feel" right to you, trust your instincts. If not, no matter how well appointed the practice may appear to be, visit more clinics before making a decision.

First Visit to the Vet

When you are comfortable with a vet practice, schedule a second visit to include your Chow puppy. Bring all the dog's medical records. Be ready to discuss completing vaccinations and having the animal spayed or neutered.

Routine exam procedures include temperature and a check of heart and lung function with a stethoscope. The vet will weigh and measure the puppy. These baseline numbers will help chart growth and physical progress. If you have specific questions, prepare them in advance.

One specific health-related tip from breeder Tammy Tosh of Hsot Chow Chows is as follows: "Chows are very hot natured – most veterinarians will apply a heating pad after surgeries and are not aware that this can cause a Chow stress. I always emphasize to remove all sources of heat from my dogs. Chows do not generally do well in a hospital setting, and it is best to remove them as soon as it is safe to do so."

Vaccinations

A puppy's recommended vaccinations begin at 6-7 weeks of age. The first injection covers distemper, hepatitis, parvovirus, parainfluenza, and coronavirus.

Boosters are set for 9, 12, and 16 weeks. In some areas, a vaccine for Lyme disease starts at 16 weeks with a booster at 18 weeks. The rabies vaccination is administered at 12-16 weeks and then generally every 3 years.

Margit Lassen of Chow Chow of Peking has this advice: "Vaccinations should only be done as a puppy 3 times and a booster shot at 1 1/2 years, and that is all. Today, all dogs are over vaccinated, but it is of course good business for the vets. Trials show that a dog that was only vaccinated as puppy still had antibodies against the major diseases at age 8."

Evaluating for Worms

Puppies purchased from a breeder are almost always parasite free. Worms are more common in rescue dogs and strays. Roundworms appear as small white granules around the anus. Other types of worms can only be seen through a microscope.

These tests are important since some parasites, like tapeworms, may be life threatening. Before a puppy's first visit, the vet will ask for a fecal sample for this purpose. If the puppy tests positive, the standard treatment is a deworming agent with a follow-up dose in 10 days.

It's best to take a stool sample at around 6-7 weeks to determine if the dog has worms or giardia. When the results are negative, it is not necessary to de-worm them. Some breeders just give them deworming medicine routinely. It's very important a fecal sample be obtaining and sent to a recognized lab for testing.

Spaying and Neutering

As discussed earlier, the Chow is a slow maturing breed, taking up to 18 months to fully mature. Spaying and neutering too early can lead to health issues.

Vancie Drew of Mei-Lings Chow Chows says: "There are many articles about the risks involved and many health issues from spaying and neutering too early. They need those hormones in order to have proper growth. I saw X-rays of a year-old Chow female who was suffering from bone density loss, and she had been spayed by 4 months of age and never allowed to have even one heat cycle, which they do need to have."

Once they do have the operation, the procedures carry health and behavioral benefits:

Neutering reduces the risk of prostatic disease or perianal tumors in male dogs. The surgery lessens aggressive behaviors, territorial instincts, urine marking, and inappropriate mounting.

Spayed females have a diminished risk for breast cancer and no prospect of uterine or ovarian cancer. There are no mood swings related to hormones or issues around the dog coming into season.

"Normal" Health Issues

Although Chow Chows are vigorous, healthy dogs, all canines can face medical issues. The following are "normal" health-related matters that may need veterinary evaluation.

Pets that are inattentive or lethargic and that are not eating or drinking should be examined. None of these behaviors is normal for a Chow.

Diarrhea

All puppies are subject to digestive upsets when they get into things they shouldn't, like human food or even the kitchen garbage, but this is less a problem with Chows than other breeds. If, however, your puppy does eat something that irritates his stomach, the resulting diarrhea should resolve within 24 hours.

During that time, the puppy should have only small portions of dry food and no treats. Give the dog lots of fresh, clean water to guard against dehydration. If the loose, watery stools are still present after 24 hours, take your Chow to the vet.

The same period of watchful waiting applies for adult dogs. If episodic diarrhea becomes chronic, take a careful look at your pet's diet.

Chances are good the dog is getting too much rich, fatty food and needs less fat and protein. Some dogs also do better eating small amounts of food several times a day rather than being offered 2-3 larger meals.

Allergy testing can identify the causes of some cases of diarrhea. Many dogs are allergic to chicken and turkey. A change in diet resolves their gastrointestinal upset immediately. Diets based on rabbit or duck are often used for dogs with such intolerances.

Either a bacteria or a virus can cause diarrhea, which accompanies fever and vomiting. Parasites, in particular tapeworms and roundworms, may also be to blame.

Photo Credit: Caryl Myers of Cejam Chows

Vomiting

Dietary changes or the puppy "getting into something" can also cause vomiting. Again, this should resolve within 24 hours. If the dog tries to vomit but can't bring anything up, vomits blood, or can't keep water down, take your pet to the vet immediately.

Dehydration from vomiting occurs faster than in a case of diarrhea, and can be fatal. It is possible that your dog may need intravenous fluids.

When your dog is vomiting, always have a good look around to identify what, if anything, the dog may have chewed and swallowed. This can be a huge benefit in targeting appropriate treatment.

Other potential culprits include: hookworm, roundworm, pancreatitis, diabetes, thyroid disease, kidney disease, liver disease, or a physical blockage.

Bloat

Any dog can suffer from bloat. The condition is the second most common cause of death in dogs behind accidental trauma (like being struck by a car) in young dogs and cancer in elderly canines.

Some breeds are at higher risk than others. Also known as gastric dilation / volvulus or GDV, bloat cannot be treated with an antibiotic or prevented with a vaccine. In roughly 50% of cases, bloat is fatal.

In severe cases, the stomach twists partially or completely. This causes circulation problems throughout the digestive system. Dogs that do not receive treatment go into cardiac arrest. Even if surgical intervention is attempted, there is no guarantee of success.

Signs of bloat are often mistaken for indications of excess gas. The dog may salivate and attempt to vomit, pace, and whine. Gas reduction products at this stage can be helpful. As the stomach swells, it places pressure on surrounding vital organs, and may burst.

All cases of bloat are a *serious* medical emergency.

Risk Factors

Larger dogs with deep chests and small waists face a greater risk of developing bloat. These include the Chow, Great Dane, Weimaraner, Saint Bernard, Irish Setter, and the Standard

Poodle.

Eating habits also factor into the equation. Dogs that eat one large meal per day consisting of dry food are in a high-risk category as well. Feed three small meals throughout the day. This helps to prevent gulping, which leads to ingesting large amounts of air.

Experts recommend dry food for dogs, but don't let your pet drink lots of water after eating. Doing so causes the dry food in the stomach to expand, leading to discomfort, and a dilution of the digestive juices.

Limit the amount of play and exercise after meals. A slow walk promotes digestion, but a vigorous romp can be dangerous. The Chow's low exercise needs are to his advantage in this regard.

Stress also contributes to bloat, especially in anxious or nervous dogs. Changes in routine, confrontations with other dogs, and moving to a new home can all trigger an attack.

Dogs between the ages of 4 and 7 are at an increased risk. Bloat occurs most often between 2 a.m. and 6 a.m., roughly 10 hours after the animal has had his dinner.

Prevention

Feed your pet small meals 2-3 times a day, limiting both water intake and exercise after eating. Take up your pet's water at mealtime, and do not offer it to the dog for at least 30 minutes after your pet finishes his meal. Do not allow strenuous activity for at least an hour.

Test your dog's dry food by putting a serving in a bowl with water. Leave the material to expand overnight. If the degree of added bulk seems excessive, consider switching to a premium or organic food.

Keep an anti-gas medicine with simethicone on hand. (Consult with your veterinarian on correct dosage.) Consider adding a probiotic to your dog's food to reduce gas in the stomach and to improve digestive health.

If a dog experiences bloat once, his risk of a future episode is greater. Keep copies of his medical records at home, and know the location of the nearest emergency vet clinic.

Allergies

Like humans, dogs suffer from allergies. Food, airborne particles, and materials that touch the skin can all cause negative reactions.

In dogs with thick coats like the Chow, hot spots may develop as a consequence of poor grooming and are often mistaken as an allergic reaction. You must make sure to thoroughly rinse your pet after a bath to prevent this from occurring.

Owners tend to notice a potential allergy when something changes in the dog's behavior to suggest discomfort like itching. Common allergy symptoms include chewing or biting of the tail, stomach, or hind legs, or licking of the paws.

In reaction to inhaled substances, the dog will sneeze, cough, or experience watering eyes. Ingested substances may lead to vomiting or diarrhea. Dogs can also suffer from rashes or a case of hives. Your poor Chow can be just as miserable as you are during an allergy attack.

If the reaction occurs in the spring or fall, the likely culprit is seasonal pollen, or, in the case of hot weather, fleas. Food additives like beef, corn, wheat, soybeans, and dairy products can all cause gastrointestinal upset.

As with any allergy, take away suspect items or try a special diet. Allergy testing offers a definitive diagnosis and pinpoints necessary environmental and dietary changes. The tests are expensive, costing $200+ / £120+.

The vet may recommend medication or bathing the dog in cool, soothing water. Special diets are also extremely helpful. For acne-like chin rashes, switch to stainless steel, glass, or ceramic food dishes. Plastic feeding dishes cause this rash, which looks like blackheads surrounded by inflamed skin. Wash the dog's face in clear, cool water and ask the vet for an antibiotic cream to speed the healing process.

General Signs of Illness

Any of the following symptoms can point to a serious medical problem. Have your pet evaluated for any of these behaviors. Don't wait out of fear that you are just being an alarmist. Vets can resolve most medical problems in dogs if treatment starts at the first sign of illness.

Coughing and/or Wheezing

Occasional coughing is not a cause for concern, but if it goes on for more than a week, a vet visit is in order. A cough may indicate:

- kennel cough
- heartworm
- cardiac disease

- bacterial infections
- parasites
- tumors
- allergies

The upper respiratory condition called "kennel cough" presents with a dry, hacking cough. It is a form of canine bronchitis caused by warm, overcrowded conditions with poor ventilation. In most cases, kennel cough resolves on its own.

Consult with your veterinarian. The doctor may prescribe a cough suppressant or suggest the use of a humidifier to soothe your pet's irritated airways.

When the cause of a cough is unclear, the vet will take a full medical history and order tests, including blood work and X-rays. Fluid may also be drawn from the lungs for analysis. Among other conditions, the doctor will be attempting to rule out heartworms.

Heartworms

Mosquitos spread heartworms (*Dirofilaria Immitis*) through their bites. They are thin, long parasites that infest the muscles of the heart, where they block blood vessels and cause bleeding. Their presence can lead to heart failure and death. Coughing and fainting, as well as an intolerance to exercise are all symptoms of heartworm. Discuss heartworm prevention with your vet and decide on the best course of action to keep your pet safe.

Other Warning Signs

Often, the signs of serious illness are subtle. Trust your

instincts. If you think something is wrong, do not hesitate to consult with your vet. Warning signs include:

- Excessive and unexplained drooling
- Excessive consumption of water and increased urination
- Changes in appetite leading to weight gain or loss
- Marked change in levels of activity
- Disinterest in favorite activities
- Stiffness and difficulty standing or climbing stairs
- Sleeping more than normal
- Shaking of the head
- Any sores, lumps, or growths
- Dry, red, or cloudy eyes

Diabetes

Canines can suffer from three types of diabetes: *insipidus*, *diabetes mellitus*, and gestational diabetes. All point to malfunctioning endocrine glands and are often linked to poor diet. Larger dogs are in a higher risk category.

- In cases of *diabetes insipidus*, low levels of the hormone vasopressin create problems with the regulation of blood glucose, salt, and water.

- *Diabetes mellitus* is more common and dangerous. It is divided into Types I and II. The first develops in young dogs and may be referred to as "juvenile." Type II is more prevalent in adult and older dogs. All cases are treated with insulin.

- Gestational diabetes occurs in pregnant female dogs and requires the same treatment as diabetes mellitus. Obese dogs are at greater risk.

Abnormal insulin levels interfere with blood sugar levels. Any dog that is obese is at a higher risk for developing diabetes.

Symptoms of Canine Diabetes

All of the following behaviors are signs that a dog is suffering from canine diabetes:

- Excessive water consumption
- Excessive and frequent urination
- Lethargy / uncharacteristic laziness
- Weight gain or loss for no reason

It is possible your pet may display no symptoms whatsoever. Diabetes can be slow to develop, so the effects may not be immediately noticeable. Regular check-ups help to catch this disease, which can be fatal.

Managing Diabetes

As part of a diabetes management program, the vet will recommend diet changes, including special food. Your dog may need insulin injections. Although this may sound daunting, your vet will train you to administer the shots. A dog with diabetes can live a full and normal life. Expect regular visits to the vet to check for heart and circulatory problems.

Hemorrhagic Gastroenteritis

Any dog can develop hemorrhagic gastroenteritis (HGE). The condition has a high mortality rate. Unfortunately, most dog owners have never heard of HGE. If a dog does not receive immediate treatment, the animal may well die.

Symptoms include:

- Profuse vomiting
- Depression
- Bloody diarrhea with a foul odor
- Severe low blood volume resulting in fatal shock within 24 hours

The exact cause of HGE is unknown, and it often occurs in otherwise healthy dogs. The average age of onset is 2-4 years. Approximately 15% of dogs that survive an attack will suffer a relapse. There is no definitive list of high-risk breeds.

The instant your dog vomits or passes blood, get your dog to the vet. Tests will rule out viral or bacterial infections, ulcers, parasites, cancer, and poisoning. X-rays and an electrocardiogram are also primary diagnostic tools for HGE.

Hospitalization and aggressive treatment are necessary. The dog will likely need IV fluids and even a blood transfusion. Both steroids and antibiotics prevent infection. If the dog survives, the animal should eat a bland diet for a week or more with only a gradual reintroduction of normal foods. In almost all cases, the dog will eat a special diet for life with the use of a probiotic.

The acute phases of HGE lasts 2-3 days. With quick and aggressive treatment, many dogs recover well. Delayed intervention for any reason means the outlook is not good.

Dental Care

Chewing is a dog's only means of maintaining his teeth. Many of our canine friends develop dental problems early in life because they don't get enough of this activity. Not all dogs are prone to cavities. Most do suffer from accumulations of plaque and associated gum diseases. Often severe halitosis (bad breath) is the first sign that something is wrong.

With dental problems, gingivitis develops first and, if unaddressed, progresses to periodontitis. Warning signs of gum disease include:

- Reluctance to finish meals
- Extreme bad breath
- Swollen and bleeding gums
- Irregular gum line
- Plaque build-up
- Drooling and/or loose teeth

The bacterial gum infection periodontitis causes inflammation, gum recession, and possible tooth loss. It requires treatment with antibiotics to prevent a spread of the infection to other parts of the body. Symptoms include:

- Pus at the gum line
- Loss of appetite
- Depression
- Irritability
- Pawing at the mouth
- Trouble chewing
- Loose or missing teeth
- Gastrointestinal upset

Treatment begins with a professional cleaning. This procedure may also involve root work, descaling, and even extractions.

With Proliferating Gum Disease, the gums overgrow the teeth causing inflammation and infection. Other symptoms include:

- Thickening and lengthening of the gums
- Bleeding
- Bad breath
- Drooling
- Loss of appetite

The vet will prescribe antibiotics, and surgery is usually required.

Home Dental Care

There are many products available to help with home dental care for your Chow. Some owners opt for water additives that break up tarter and plaque, but such products may cause stomach upset. Dental sprays and wipes are also an option, but so is gentle gum massage to help break up plaque and tarter.

Most owners incorporate some type of dental chew in their standard care practices. Greenies Dental Chews for Dogs are popular and well tolerated in a digestive sense. An added plus is that dogs usually love them. The treats come in different sizes and are priced in a range of $7 / £4.21 for 22 "Teeny Greenies" and $25 / £15 for 17 Large Greenies.

Brushing your pet's teeth is the ultimate defense for oral health. This involves the use of both a canine-specific toothbrush and toothpaste. Never use human toothpaste, which contains fluoride toxic to your dog. Some dog toothbrushes resemble smaller versions of our own, but I like the models that just fit over your fingertip. I think they offer greater control and stability.

The real trick to brushing your pet's teeth is getting the dog comfortable with having your hands in his mouth. Start by just massaging the dog's face, and then progressing to the gums before using the toothbrush. In the beginning, you can even just smear the toothpaste on the teeth with your fingertip.

Try to schedule these brushing sessions for when the dog is a little tired, perhaps after a long walk. Don't apply pressure, which can stress the dog. Just move in small circular motions and stop when the Chow has had enough of the whole business. If you don't feel you've done enough, stop. A second session is better than forcing your dog to do something he doesn't like and creating a negative association in his mind.

Even if you do practice a full home dental care routine, don't scrimp on annual oral exams in the vet's office. Exams not only help to keep the teeth and gums healthy, but also to check for the presence of possible cancerous growths.

Canine Eye Care

Check your dog's eyes on a regular schedule to avoid problems like clogged tear ducts. Many dogs also suffer from excessive tearing, which can stain the fur around the eyes and down the muzzle.

As a part of good grooming, keep the corners of your pet's eyes and the muzzle free of mucus to prevent bacterial growth. If your dog is prone to mucus accumulation, ask your vet for sterile eyewash or gauze pads. In addition, consider having the dog tested for environmental allergies.

With longhaired animals, take the precaution of keeping the hair well-trimmed around your pet's eyes. If you do not feel comfortable doing this chore yourself, discuss the problem with your groomer. Shorter hair prevents the transference of bacteria and avoids trauma from scrapes and scratches.

Dogs love to hang their heads out of car windows, but this can result in eye injuries and serious infection from blowing debris. If you don't want to deprive your dog of this simple pleasure, I recommend a product called Doggles.

These protective goggles for dogs come in a range of colors and sizes for less than $20 / £12 per pair. The investment in protecting your dog's eyes is well worth it. All my pets have worn the Doggles without complaint.

Conjunctivitis

Conjunctivitis is the most common eye infection seen in dogs. It presents with redness around the eyes and a green or yellow discharge. Antibiotics will treat the infection. The dreaded "cone of shame" collar then prevents more injury from scratching during healing.

Entropion

Entropion is a condition in which the dog's eyelid turns inward, irritating the cornea. The issue becomes apparent in puppies with squinting and excessive tearing. In most cases, the condition resolves as the dog ages.

In severe instances, a canine ophthalmologist must tack the lids with stitches that will remain in place for a period of days or weeks until the correct "fit" is achieved. During healing, artificial tears are used to prevent drying of the eyes.

Wendy Nieminen and Pete Dingwell of Bearcrest Chows share their personal experience: "Chows are prone to Eye Entropion because of their almond shaped eye, and it is very common in this breed as well as some others. It is fixable by a simple eye surgery down the road. A lot of times this will pop up during different stages of growth up until 18 months of age. It can disappear just as quick. DO NOT let your vet talk you into having surgery too soon. Some will even try to get you to do it at 6 months of age. They are not done growing and have a lot of excess skin yet.

"Check their eyes and if you notice tearing or discharge, pick up some optimyacin or polysporin eye ointment and put a bit in one to two times a day. It keeps the eye lubricated (to avoid scratching the cornea and to get rid of any infection). Another good thing to have on hand is Swanson's Sterile Eye Lubricant. It is just a lubricant and does not contain any antibiotics, so it can be used as often as necessary to get them through these times.

"There are other things you can do to help, as well. Sometimes massaging the eyes daily by pulling the lower lids down and upper lid up, will make a difference. Cleaning the fur around the outside of the eye with a diluted solution of plain Listerine on a cotton ball can kill any bacteria living on the fur, keeping it from growing and spreading. Do not get it anywhere near the eye rim or in the eye!

"Another option if it seems quite bad is the vet can just put a small stitch or tack under the eye to keep the lashes from rubbing until the dog is older. Usually by 18 months of age, the head of the Chow has filled out and the problem is gone. If surgery is done too soon, the head of the Chow fills out, and the dog will end up with a "deer caught in the headlights look" (too wide eyed). They also may develop the opposite problem where the eye is pulled open too much from the early surgery and dirt and debris can get in and cause infections. So it is important to try to wait out the growing stages if possible and make sure all other options are looked at, before going ahead with any surgery."

Cherry Eye

The condition called "cherry eye" is an irritation of the third eyelid. It appears as a bright pink protrusion in the corner of the eye. Either injury or a bacterial infection causes cherry eye. It may occur in one or both eyes and requires surgery to effect a permanent cure.

The Matter of Genetic Abnormalities

The Chow is a hardy dog with only a few common health problems including: hip and elbow dysplasia, patellar luxation, autoimmune thyroiditis, cataracts, distichiasis, and glaucoma. I have discussed bloat and gastric torsion, which is seen in the breed. An autoimmune skin disease, pemphigus foliaceous, may also be present in Chows, as well as melanoma.

Canine Arthritis

Dogs, like humans, can suffer from arthritis, which may develop in the presence of hip or elbow dysplasia as a secondary complication. Arthritis is a debilitating degeneration of the joints and is common in larger breeds.

As the cartilage in the joints breaks down, the action of bone rubbing on bone creates considerable pain. In turn, the animal's range of motion becomes restricted.

Standard treatments do not differ from those used for humans. Aspirin addresses pain and inflammation, while supplements like glucosamine work on improving joint health. Environmental aids, like steps and ramps, ease the strain on the affected joints and help pets stay active.

Arthritis also occurs as a natural consequence of aging. Management focuses on making your pet comfortable and facilitating ease of motion. Some dogs become so crippled that their humans buy mobility carts for them.

Hip and Elbow Dysplasia

Chows are susceptible to hip and elbow dysplasia. This defect prevents the leg bones from fitting properly into the hip joint. It is a painful condition that causes limping in the hind or forequarters. The condition may be inherited or the consequence of injury and aging.

The standard treatment is anti-inflammatory medication. Some cases need surgery and even a full joint replacement. Surgical intervention for this defect carries a high success rate, allowing your dog to live a full and happy life.

Luxating Patella

A dog with a luxating patella experiences frequent dislocations of the kneecap. The condition can affect one or both kneecaps. Surgery may be required to rectify the problem. Often owners have no idea anything is wrong with their dog's knee joint. Then the pet jumps off a bed or leaps to catch a toy, lands badly, and begins to limp and favor the leg. The condition may be genetic in origin, so it is important to ask a breeder owner if the problem has surfaced in the line of dogs he cultivates. A luxating patella can also be the consequence of a physical injury, especially as a dog ages.

Any time you see your dog limping or seeming more fatigued

than usual after exercise, have the dog checked out. Conditions like a luxating patella only get worse with time and wear, and need immediate treatment.

Photo Credit: Wendy Nieminen & Pete Dingwell of Bearcrest Chows

Autoimmune Thyroiditis

In cases of autoimmune thyroiditis, the dog's immune system develops antibodies against the body's own thyroid gland, attacking and destroying the cells. The surviving cells then must worker harder to compensate.

At the point at which 75% of the thyroid gland is destroyed, the dog will begin to display signs of hypothyroidism. Recent studies have found autoimmune thyroiditis to be the leading cause of canine hypothyroidism.

The symptoms of hypothyroidism in dogs include:

- Lethargy
- Weight gain
- Dulling of the coat
- Skin infections
- Diarrhea or constipation
- Intolerance to cold
- Changes to the skin (odor, greasiness, or dryness)
- Behavioral changes, including aggression and increased reactivity
- Furrowing of the skin on the forehead

Outpatient management of hyperthyroidism with medication is generally effective.

Cataracts

Aging dogs often develop cataracts, which is a clouding of the lens of the eye leading to blurred vision. The lesion can vary in size and will be visible as a blue-gray area. In most cases, the vet will watch but not treat cataracts. The condition does not affect your pet's life in a severe way. Dogs adapt well to the senses they do have, so diminished vision is not as problematic as it would be for us.

Distichiasis

A "distichia" is an eyelash that grows from an abnormal place on the eyelid or in an abnormal direction. This may occur on the upper or lower lid. Usually more than one is present; the plural is distichiae. This condition is similar to entropion.

If sufficiently severe, the abnormal eyelashes scratch the cornea, causing ulceration. The eye and or conjunctiva may be red and inflamed.

Discharge can be present and the animal may blink excessively, squinting from pain and keeping the eye closed. If ulceration has developed, the affected cornea will appear to be bluish. Mild cases may require no treatment, or the simple use of lubricating drops. Severe cases must be addressed with corrective surgery, but in such instances, the prognosis is excellent.

Glaucoma

With glaucoma, increased pressure prevents proper drainage of fluid. Glaucoma may develop on its own, or as a complication of a shifted cataract. Dogs with glaucoma experience partial or total loss of vision within one year of diagnosis. Symptoms include swelling, excessive tearing, redness, and evident visual limitations. Suspected glaucoma requires immediate medical attention.

Pemphigus Foliaceous

"Pemphigus" refers to a group of autoimmune skin diseases. All cause the skin to crust and ulcerate along with the presence of sacs of fluid, cysts, and pustules. Four types affect dogs: pemphigus foliaceous, pemphigus erythematosus, pemphigus vulgaris, and pemphigus vegetans.

The symptoms of pemphigus foliaceous include:

- Scaly, itchy red skin with pustules, crusting, and shallow ulcers
- Overgrowth and cracking of the footpads, causing lameness
- Sacs of fluid in the skin
- Swollen lymph glands

The areas of the body most commonly affected are the head, ears, and pads, with spread to the lips and gums possible. The affected dog may be healthy otherwise, but experience varying degrees of pain and discomfort depending on the severity of the breakdown of the skin. There is also a danger of secondary bacterial infection.

Dogs suffering from pemphigus foliaceous typically require hospitalization for supportive care. The vet will likely use steroid therapy to bring the condition under control in concert with a low-fat diet to avoid a danger of pancreatitis.

When the dog is able to go home, follow-up appointments occur weekly with blood work performed until the condition has gone into remission. Since exposure to the sun can worsen the condition, the dog should be kept indoors.

Melanoma

Melanoma is the most common oral tumor in dogs, and it can also occur on the toes. Male dogs are more likely to develop this form of cancer, which is seen most often in Chow Chows, Golden Retrievers, Scottish Terriers, Cocker Spaniels, and Gordon Setters.

Such tumors are locally invasive and infiltrate into the bone with a high rate of metastasis. Treatment depends entirely on location. Tumors on the toes are generally amputated along with the digit itself, but the removal of oral tumors may affect the dog's ability to eat.

Both radiation and chemotherapy may be attempted. Untreated, the dog will die in a matter of months. With early detection and treatment, life expectancy is 1.5-2 years.

Breeding Chow Chows

The decision to breed a dog like the Chow should only be undertaken for one reason — a desire to improve existing bloodlines mixed with a healthy love for these exceptional animals. Breeding pedigreed dogs is not a get-rich quick scheme, nor is it an inexpensive hobby. Before you even contemplate making such a commitment to living creatures, you must be an expert not only in living with and training Chows, but also in reliably pairing animals for the best genetic results.

Becoming a top breeder is a long but rewarding road. Like anything worth doing or having, there is a great deal of effort involved. Begin by attending dog shows to see "show" examples of the breed and to get to know some of the breeders. As show folks start to see you on a regular basis, more doors will begin to open up. You may then be able to get your foundation dogs.

If you do it right, don't expect to make money. Most breeders are happy if they break even at the end of any given year. Start with the best dogs you can find because, if you don't, you will always be playing catch up with your breeding program. Health-test your dogs to make sure you are raising dogs that conform to the standard but are also healthy. There are too many dogs with health problems as it is.

The purpose of this book is not to educate potential breeders, but to introduce the Chow to potential owners. You have a great deal to learn before you can even consider becoming a breeder, but if that is your ultimate goal, start making friends in the Chow world now. Cultivating a mentor is an essential step toward owning and operating a successful, well-run breeding operation.

Chapter 9 – Chow Chows and Aging

It can be heartbreaking to watch your beloved pet grow older – he may develop health problems like arthritis, and he simply might not be as active as he once was.

Unfortunately, aging is a natural part of life that cannot be avoided. All you can do is learn how to provide for your Chow Chow's needs as he ages so you can keep him with you for as long as possible.

Photo Credit: Minnie & Paul Odenkirchen of Mi Pao Kennels - This is Can. & Am. CH.MI-PAO'S THOR, a male @ 8 ½ years of age, who has been a multiple BIS winner.

What to Expect

Aging is a natural part of life for both humans and dogs. Sadly, dogs reach the end of their lives sooner than most humans do.

Once your Chow Chow reaches the age of 8 years or so, he

can be considered a "senior" dog.

At this point, you may need to start feeding him a dog food specially formulated for older dogs, and you may need to take some other precautions as well.

In order to properly care for your Chow as he ages, you might find it helpful to know what to expect. On this page, you will find a list of things to expect as your Chow Chow dog starts to get older:

• Your dog may be less active than he was in his youth – he will likely still enjoy walks, but he may not last as long as he once did, and he might take it at a slower pace.

• Your Chow Chow's joints may start to give him trouble – check for signs of swelling and stiffness, and consult your veterinarian with any problems.

• Your Chow may sleep more than he once did – this is a natural sign of aging, but it can also be a symptom of a health problem, so consult your vet if your dog's sleeping becomes excessive.

• He may have a greater tendency to gain weight, so you will need to carefully monitor his diet to keep him from becoming obese in his old age.

• He may have trouble walking or jumping, so keep an eye on your Chow Chow if he has difficulty jumping, or if he starts dragging his back feet.

• Your Chow Chow's vision may no longer be as sharp as it once was, so he may be predisposed to these problems.

•   You may need to trim your Chow Chow's nails more frequently if he doesn't spend as much time outside as he once did when he was younger.

•   He may be more sensitive to extreme heat and cold, so make sure he has a comfortable place to lie down both inside and outside.

•   Your Chow will develop gray hair around the face and muzzle – this may be less noticeable in Chows with a lighter coat.

While many of the signs mentioned above are natural side effects of aging, they can also be symptoms of serious health conditions.

If your Chow develops any of these problems suddenly, consult your veterinarian immediately.

Caring for an Older Chow Chow

When your Chow Chow gets older, he may require different care than he did when he was younger.

The more you know about what to expect as your Chow Chow ages, the better equipped you will be to provide him with the care he needs to remain healthy and mobile.

Here are some tips for caring for your Chow as he ages:

•   Schedule routine annual visits with your veterinarian to make sure your Chow Chow is in good condition.

•   Consider switching to a dog food that is specially formulated for senior dogs – a food that is too high in calories may cause your dog to gain weight.

• Supplement your dog's diet with DHA and EPA fatty acids to help prevent joint stiffness and arthritis.

• Brush your Chow Chow's teeth regularly to prevent periodontal diseases, which are fairly common in older dogs.

• Continue to exercise your dog on a regular basis – he may not be able to move as quickly, but you still need to keep him active to maintain joint and muscle health.

• Provide your Chow with soft bedding on which to sleep – the hard floor may aggravate his joints and worsen arthritis.

• Use ramps to get your dog into the car and onto the bed, if he is allowed, because he may no longer be able to jump.

• Consider putting down carpet or rugs on hard floors – slippery hardwood or tile flooring can be very problematic for arthritic dogs.

In addition to taking some of the precautions listed above in caring for your elderly Chow Chow, you may want to familiarize yourself with some of the health conditions your dog is likely to develop in his old age.

Elderly dogs are also likely to exhibit certain changes in behavior, including:

• Confusion or disorientation
• Increased irritability
• Decreased responsiveness to commands

- Increase in vocalization (barking, whining, etc.)
- Heightened reaction to sound
- Increased aggression or protectiveness
- Changes in sleep habits
- Increase in house soiling accidents

As he ages, these tendencies may increase – he may also become more protective of you around strangers.

As your Chow Chow gets older, you may find that he responds to your commands even less frequently than he used to.

The most important thing you can do for your senior dog is to schedule regular visits with your veterinarian. You should also, however, keep an eye out for signs of disease as your dog ages.

The following are common signs of disease in elderly dogs:

- Decreased appetite
- Increased thirst and urination
- Difficulty urinating/constipation
- Blood in the urine
- Difficulty breathing/coughing
- Vomiting or diarrhea
- Poor coat condition

If you notice your elderly Chow exhibiting any of these symptoms, you would be wise to seek veterinary care for your dog as soon as possible.

Euthanasia

The hardest decision any dog owner makes is helping a

suffering animal to pass easily and humanely. I have been in this position, and even though I know my beloved companied died peacefully and with no pain, my own anguish was considerable. Thankfully, I was in the care of and accepting the advice and counsel of exceptional veterinary professionals.

This is the crucial component in the decision to euthanize an animal. For your own peace of mind, you must know that you have been given the best medical advice possible. My vet was not only knowledgeable and patient, but she was kind and forthright. I valued all of those qualities and hope you are as blessed as I was in the same situation.

But the bottom line is this. No one is in a position to judge you. You must make the best decision that you can for your pet and for yourself. So long as you are acting from a position of love, respect, and responsibility, whatever you do is "right."

Grieving a Lost Pet

Some humans have difficulty fully recognizing the terrible grief involved in losing a beloved canine friend.

There will be many who do not understand the close bond we humans can have with our dogs, which is often unlike any we have with our human counterparts.

Your friends may give you pitying looks and try to cheer you up, but if they have never experienced the loss of such a special connection themselves, they may also secretly think you are making too much fuss over "just a dog."

For some of us humans, the loss of a beloved dog is so painful that we decide never to share our lives with another, because the thought of going through the pain of such a loss is unbearable.

Expect to feel terribly sad, tearful, and yes, depressed, because those who are close to their canine companions will feel their loss no less acutely than the loss of a human friend or life partner.

The grieving process can take some time to recover from, and some of us never totally recover.

After the loss of a family dog, first you need to take care of yourself by making certain that you remember to eat regular meals and get enough sleep, even though you will feel an almost eerie sense of loneliness.

Losing a beloved dog is a shock to the system that can also affect your concentration and your ability to find joy or be interested in participating in other activities that are a normal part of your daily life.

Other dogs, cats, and pets in the home will also be grieving the loss of a companion and may display this by acting depressed, being off their food, or showing little interest in play or games.

Therefore, you need to help guide your other pets through this grieving process by keeping them busy and interested, taking them for extra walks, and finding ways to spend more time with them.

Wait Long Enough

Many people do not wait long enough before attempting to

replace a lost pet and will immediately go to the local shelter and rescue a deserving dog. While this may help to distract you from your grieving process, this is not really fair to the new fur member of your family.

Bringing a new pet into a home that is depressed and grieving the loss of a long-time canine member may create behavioral problems for the new dog that will be faced with learning all about their new home, while also dealing with the unstable energy of the grieving family.

A better scenario would be to allow yourself the time to properly grieve by waiting a minimum of one month to allow yourself and your family to feel happier and more stable before deciding upon sharing your home with another dog.

Insurance Costs

Thanks to advances in veterinary science, our pets now receive viable and effective treatments. The estimated annual cost for a medium-sized dog, including health care, is $650 / £387. (This does not include emergency care, advanced procedures, or consultations with specialists.)

The growing interest in pet insurance to help defray these costs is understandable. You can buy a policy covering accidents, illness, and hereditary and chronic conditions for $25 / £16.25 per month. Benefit caps and deductibles vary by company. To get rate quotes, investigate the following companies in the United States and the UK:

United States of America

http://www.24PetWatch.com
http://www.ASPCAPetInsurance.com

http://www.EmbracePetInsurance.com
http://www.PetsBest.com
http://www.PetInsurance.com

United Kingdom

http://www.Animalfriends.org.uk
http://www.Healthy-pets.co.uk
http://www.Petplan.co.uk

Afterword

The Chow is a perfect example of a breed that has long
suffered from an undeserved reputation. Because the dogs
became popular so rapidly after they were introduced in
Great Britain and the United States, puppy mills heavily
targeted Chows. This led to litters produced with no
conscious cultivation of genetic quality and temperament.

Photo Credit: Linda Fernandez of Cherub Chows, BISS A/C Ch.
Cherub Thunder of The Lords

Although dedicated breeders have worked tirelessly to produce animals that are superior and reliable companions, Chows still labor under this stereotype. I fell for it too, initially reacting to one of the most beautifully behaved animals I have ever known with fear and suspicion.

I'm very glad that my friend's dog Penny was in my life for the time I knew her. She was an intelligent, intuitive creature who gave Sandy years of loyalty and unquestioning devotion. The fact that Penny came to see me as someone who was acceptable in her world was a tremendous compliment.

I did have many thoughtful conversations with her. She listened gravely to my every word, and I'm sorry she lacked the voice to tell me what she was thinking, because she clearly was doing just that.

If you decide to welcome a Chow into your life, prepare to be ruined for any other breed. This is what happened to Sandy. Ten years after Penny's death, my friend still has not adopted another dog. But at the same time, get ready for a once-in-a-lifetime experience with a loyal and devoted companion animal. For all her grief over the loss of Penny, Sandy refers to the Chow as one of the great loves of her life.

This is a common theme among Chow owners and is the joy of owning the breed. Although the myth that the dogs are descended from some extinct species of bear is just that, a myth, it is true that no other breed is quite like the somber and enigmatic Chow Chow.

Bonus Chapter 1 - Interview With Tiffany Maddux

Can you tell us who you are and where you are based?

My name is Tiffany Maddux and I run RHR Chow Chow Kennel in Ava, Missouri.

What inspired you to become a breeder and how did you start with Chow Chows?

I am a licensed vet tech and worked with a client that has had RHR Kennel for about 27 years; they were looking to retire and bring in someone to take over the kennel and promote their breed the CHOW CHOW. I have been a vet tech and worked emergency, small and large animal before taking over about 2 years ago. I have been amazed at how awesome this breed truly is and feel very fortunate to have found them and have them be a part of my life.

Is it possible to describe a fairly typical Chow Chow?

A typical Chow is anything but typical in the dog world. They can be as outgoing as a lap dog, or as reserved and aloof as a king. They are very much a product of their environment. They are naturally more reserved than many breeds, but to me that is a good thing. You win them over and gain their trust and loyalty and they will cross fire for you. They are some of the most loyal dogs I have ever been around. As loyal as they are they might have days where they are very stubborn. They are not an ideal beginner dog, unless you are prepared to go to puppy classes, training, and have lots of time.

What types of people are buying Chow Chows and why?

Chows are fairly adaptable to most circumstances. Most of my Chows go to families, especially with stay at home moms, where they want a loyal family dog that will also alert them if anything is going on. I also have Chows that make great truck riding dogs, and daycare centers as they are tolerant when properly socialized. The most important thing to consider is the disposition of the Chow; not every Chow does well in every home situation. Some are more energetic and need a faster paced home, hiking, country lifestyle. I have even had these types of Chows in sled dog homes and they do well while there are other Chows that are content laying on the couch, maybe a walk to the dog park is enough excitement for them. I try to place Chows with a fitting home, and it is pretty easy to see their temperament at a young age.

Can you offer advice to people looking to buy a Chow Chow and how much should they be spending?

I always recommend finding a breeder that you can talk with and visit their kennel. I think it is very important to see where your puppy comes from, meet the breeder, and always meet the parents. You have to realize that when you go to the kennel the Chows act like Chows; they may be stoic and stand offish with new people. But they should never act aggressive. They should be at least friendly and outgoing with the breeder. If you are not able to find a local breeder, then make sure they are a licensed kennel and get some references off families that have not only visited the kennel but also had puppies shipped. As far as a price goes, that greatly depends on where you are located and what your intentions are. If you want to show your Chow, you will obviously be in a larger price range than a family pet. I only raise as family pets, although I have had my Chow Chows do well showing but that is not my motive for breeding. I would say that you can find a healthy, happy Chow puppy for anywhere from $500-

$1500. That is a large price range, but has a lot of variants.

Are there things new owners do that perhaps frustrate you?

New Chow Chow owners are great for me. They seem to be the most interested in learning about the breed and very much accepting of advice. They always try their best, keep me updated and ask questions. I love sharing my experiences not only with raising Chows, but working as a vet tech for training and advice. My only pet peeve is waiting until there is a huge behavior problem before addressing it. 100% of the time I have talked with someone about a problem, either a Chow from me or another breeder/rescue, there were a lot of little things that led up to the problem they are having. It is a lot easier to fix the little problems, than to have a fix a bigger one.

Do they attract a lot of interest and curiosity from the public?

Very much so! I don't remember taking any of my Chow Chows, whether that be adult or puppies, that it did not strike up a conversation. Usually involving childhood stories of either their Chow or a neighbor's that would protect all the neighborhood kids. I love all the stories and it gets people thinking about a breed that is not very common anymore. A few decades ago most people had a Chow in their family somewhere, today that is not so. I have also had many people ask me what they are because they have not seen them. That to me is a great opportunity to tell them what I know about the Chow.

What type of health issues can a Chow Chow have and how do you deal with preventing these?

I would say the #1 health problem in the Chow Chow is eye entropion. This is fairly common, although not allowed in my breeding Chows, it does pop up. As puppies their eyes can be tacked to relieve the eye watering that is associated with entropion, but it is very important to find an experienced veterinarian. If surgery is performed at too young of an age to correct this condition, more issues arise from taking too much skin and they can have worse eyes. If the eyes water excessively many things need to be ruled out before surgery is considered. It could be allergies, either to food or something in the environment. Carpet cleaners, perfumes, room spray, and candles can all cause allergies, which show through the skin of Chow Chows. There have been instances with hip and knee issues in the Chow, but I have not seen this as common. I always tell families to be careful and not encourage jumping off of couch, beds, off docks, etc until the growth plates have closed as it can cause arthritis later in life.

What is the typical temperament of a Chow Chow, so people know what to expect from their new pet?

The temperament of a Chow Chow is very different from most other breeds. They are independent yet loyal. The thing I really admire about the breed is their personality; they make decisions for themselves. You may be able to convince them to do something, but usually there has to be something in it for them. They are very smart and do not forget. My puppies seem to housebreak themselves and I rarely have accident problems. They do well with crate training or just a room set aside for them. If they get overwhelmed by a situation they will just walk to their area and relax for a bit. It is important to socialize but also to let them have an area that they do not have to worry about being nervous. Once they adapt to their new home it is not needed, but I also say it is a good idea, whether you have neighbor kids that run through or repair guys, that they have an area they call their own to avoid the excitement.

Do you have any special feeding routines or diet?

I free feed all of my Chow Chows – this seems to help avoid food guarding. If I have 3 Chows in the yard, I give them 4 bowls in different areas. If it is always there, they nibble throughout the day and never tend to overeat. That being said, I also have intact Chows. They exercise regularly and burn lots of calories. If you live in an apartment or have an older spayed/neutered Chow that barely goes out to potty, that may or may not work. Every dog needs a different amount of calories to sustain a good body condition. As far as diet goes, my best recommendation is to find a good quality food that has been around and not had many recalls. Chows do tend to get hot spots and have skin problems if a food is too high in corn. So I recommend a chicken and rice formula, or a lamb and sweet potato. As puppies, they need a good quality puppy chow to grow and develop as needed. Many puppy foods are not high in quality and the puppy becomes poor. I recommend talking with your breeder about brands they recommend. If they raise quality puppies, they have probably found a food they like.

What colors and sizes are most popular?

Chows come in 5 basic colors; red, black, cream, cinnamon, and blue. Cinnamon and blue are dilute colors and are produced when one parent is either a dilute, or has the genetics in their background. Dilute colors should never be bred to another dilute as it can cause pigment issues including pink tongues, blue/pink eyes, off colors, blindness, and deafness. I have families that love all 5 colors, but red and blue are usually favorites, although cream is becoming very popular.

Chow Chows can have a pretty large difference in size. Most females are 40-60 lbs, although I have many a little larger. Males tend to be 50-80 lbs, but I do have a couple that are larger. I have some families that love the smaller Chows, while others want as big as you can get! I breed for health, conformation, and temperament. Size is a plus, and I prefer the larger Chow, as they were originally a medium/large breed.

As a breed expert, are there any 'essential' tips you would like to share with new owners?

The best advice I can give to a new Chow Chow owner is to do a lot of research before buying a puppy. Talk with breeders, visit a kennel, talk and talk some more. A Chow is a commitment of at least 10-15 years. They do not rehome easily due to how strongly they bond. You must be serious about the puppy, as there is very little in the way of rescue for Chows, and most shelters do not adopt them. I guarantee all of my puppies a forever home if something does occur, but it is a very hard transition for an adult Chow. Also find a knowledgeable vet that has experience with Chows, and a trainer that has worked with them. Chow Chows are a very amazing breed and have a very long history, but is still the stoic, loyal partner that knows he/she is royalty!

Tiffany Maddux, Bob and Kathleen Twedt of RHR Chow Chows
http://www.rhrchowchow.com/

Bonus Chapter 2 - Interview With Margit Lassen

Margit, can you tell us who you are and where you live?

I am from Germany and immigrated to Canada in 1977. I live in Nova Scotia. I had a Collie kennel in Germany and showed my dogs.

Can you remember your first contact or experience with a Chow Chow?

On those dog shows, I met the Chows for the first time and was impressed with their quiet demeanor and beauty, and when we came to Canada I chose the Chow for my first dog here.

How did you get into breeding and what made you decide to concentrate on the Chow Chow?

We got our first Chow in 1978 but had to put her to sleep

when she was only 2 years old because of health reasons. So there were other dog breeds after her but in 1995 I got my first male and named him Moritz because he was black. Half a year later Maxi, a red female joined our family. And since I already bred dogs in Germany, we decided to have our first litter which arrived in April 1997. We were proud parents of 6 beautiful puppies, 5 red and one black.

How does a person start off becoming a breeder?

To become a breeder you should always inform yourself of all the health issues every breed has; with the Chows their hips, elbows, patellae, and eyes. Then get to know good breeders and talk to them, visit shows and read a lot.

Presumably there is a lot more behind the scenes than most people realize?

Yes there is and not all good and pleasant.

Would you change anything if you were able to go back in time and start over again?

Of course, I would change things because we all make mistakes. But the one thing I always would repeat is to have a Chow in my life.

What makes people enquire about a Chow over another breed of dog?

Why a Chow? For me it is easy, they are very loyal, they are quiet dogs and good watchdogs, they are beautiful and very clean, puppies are born "almost housebroken."

Do you think the breed is becoming more popular, less popular or staying the same do you think?

I think the breed is staying the same, and I am worried if the breed would become very popular because then the backyard breeding would increase too, and we end up like decades before with aggressive Chows who are the nightmare of vets.

What do you look for in a prospective owner and do you sometimes decide someone is unsuitable?

My future puppy owner must live in their own house. I never sell a puppy into apartment living. The Chow can live in an apartment no question but there is always the chance of changing, moving, landlords who do not approve a dog, etc. Also a fenced in garden or yard is a must. I prefer to sell my pups to people who have already had Chow experience, because the Chow is not an easy breed to have as a first time dog. They need an owner who is alpha and strict without harming the dog, they must be willing to groom a lot and accept that a Chow is not there to please his master always.

They have their own head and agenda. They still have hunting genes in them, some more than others, and need to be on leash most of the time. And of course I said "no" to some potential buyers. I talk to them and I need to feel a connection with them and towards the dogs.

How much do your Chows sell for?

My Chows sell for $1500 (Canadian dollars) as companion dogs and $2500 for dogs with breeding rights.

Did you ever feel tempted to get into showing Chows?

No, because I think the show "circus" is a brutal thing and a lot of backstabbing and bad mouthing is going on. I also do not want my dog on the road a lot during show season. I showed dogs in Germany and that experience was enough for me. But for people who love to travel and share their dogs with others and like to spend a lot of money it is for sure a good thing.

As a professional breeder can you give any tips to new owners, things they are unlikely to know that would be invaluable in helping them?

For new owners the most important thing is to find an honest and good breeder and to know what you want. Visit the parents if possible and look at the litter several times. A Chow is not a dog to be tied up outside, so they are buying a house companion. Chows are not toys or birthday/Christmas presents for small children. They need an experienced owner and a stable home. The Chow loves a home where things are stable and every day is the same. They hate changes and have a hard time to adjust to that.

Do you have any feeding advice or brands that you prefer?

I feed Acana grain free food. I would advise to stay away from dog foods that have corn in it and meats (chicken, beef) because that is not a good ration. In my opinion, the best food you can afford is just good enough. Chows are prone to have hot spots and a lot of those are due to poor feeding.

Are there any final thoughts that you feel the readers of this book would benefit from?

Only get a Chow if you do not want a dog that is devoted to please you – then get a German Shepherd; if you want a dog that is easily trainable, then get a poodle. If you can live with a VERY smart and intelligent dog that is also very independent, then the Chow is for you.

Margit and Bernd Lassen of Chow Chow of Peking
http://chowchowofpeking.tripod.com/

Relevant Websites

The Chow Chow Club
http://www.chowclub.org/ccci/

American Kennel Club
http://www.akc.org/dog-breeds/chow-chow/

Chow Chow Welfare Information and Adoption Center
http://www.chowwelfare.com/

New England Chow Chow Club
http://www.newenglandchowchowclub.com/

The Chow Chow Breed Council - UK
http://www.chowchowbreedcouncil.co.uk/

The Chow Chow Club (UK)
http://www.thechowchowclub.co.uk/

The Chow Chow Club of Wales
http://www.chowchowclubofwales.com/

The Chow Chow Club of Scotland
http://www.thechowchowclubofscotland.com/

Chow Chow Directory
http://www.netchows.com/

The Midland Chow Chow Club
http://www.midlandchowchowclub.com/

Northern Counties Chow Chow Club
http://www.northerncountieschowchowclub.co.uk/

The North Eastern Chow Chow Club
http://www.northeasternchowchowclub.com/

The National Chow Chow Club
http://www.nationalchowchowclub.com/

The Kennel Club
http://www.thekennelclub.org.uk/

Photo Credit: Minnie & Paul Odenkirchen of Mi Pao Kennels -
This is Norwegian Champion Rhytzo Dressed in Blue.

Glossary

Abdomen – The surface area of a dog's body lying between the chest and the hindquarters; also referred to as the belly.

Allergy – An abnormally sensitive reaction to substances including pollens, foods, or microorganisms. May be present in humans or animals with similar symptoms including, but not limited to, sneezing, itching, and skin rashes.

Anal glands – Glands located on either side of a dog's anus used to mark territory. May become blocked and require treatment by a veterinarian.

Arm – On a dog, the region between the shoulder and the elbow is referred to as the arm or the upper arm.

Back – That portion of a dog's body that extends from the withers (or shoulder) to the croup (approximately the area where the back flows into the tail.)

Backyard breeder – Any person engaged in the casual breeding of purebred dogs with no regard to genetic quality or consideration of the breed standard is referred to as a backyard breeder.

Bitch – The appropriate term for a female dog.

Blooded – An accepted reference to a pedigreed dog.

Breed – A line or race of dogs selected and cultivated by man from a common gene pool to achieve and maintain a characteristic appearance and function.

Breed standard – A written "picture" of a perfect specimen of a given breed in terms of appearance, movement, and behavior as formulated by a parent organization, for example, the American Kennel Club or in Great Britain, The Kennel Club.

Brows – The contours of the frontal bone that form ridges above a dog's eyes.

Buttocks – The hips or rump of a dog.

Castrate – The process of removing a male dog's testicles.

Chest – That portion of a dog's trunk or body encased by the ribs.

Coat – The hair covering a dog. Most breeds have both an outer coat and an undercoat.

Come into Season – The point at which a female dog becomes fertile for purposes of mating.

Congenital – Any quality, particularly an abnormality, present at birth.

Crate – Any portable container used to house a dog for transport or provided to a dog in the home as a "den."

Crossbred – Dogs are said to be crossbred when each of their parents is of a different breed.

Dam – A term for the female parent.

Dew Claw – The dew claw is an extra claw on the inside of the leg. It is a rudimentary fifth toe.

Euthanize – The act of relieving the suffering of a terminally ill animal by inducing a humane death, typically with an overdose of anesthesia.

Fancier – Any person with an exceptional interest in purebred dogs and the shows where they are exhibited.

Groom – To make a dog's coat neat by brushing, combing, or trimming.

Harness - A cloth or leather strap shaped to fit the shoulders and chest of a dog with a ring at the top for attaching a lead. An alternative to using a collar.

Haunch Bones – Terminology for the hip bones of a dog.

Haw – The membrane inside the corner of a dog's eye known as the third eyelid.

Head – The cranium and muzzle of a dog.

Hip Dysplasia – A condition in dogs due to a malformation of the hip resulting in painful and limited movement of varying degrees.

Hindquarters – The back portion of a dog's body including the pelvis, thighs, hocks, and paws.

Hock – Bones on the hind leg of a dog that form the joint between the second thigh and the metatarsus. Known as the dog's true heel.

Inbreeding – When two dogs of the same breed that are closely related mate.

Lead – Any strap, cord, or chain used to restrain or lead a dog. Typically attached to a collar or harness. Also called a leash.

Litter – The puppy or puppies from a single birth or "whelping."

Muzzle – That portion of a dog's head lying in front of the eyes and consisting of the nasal bone, nostrils, and jaws.

Neuter – To castrate or spay a dog thus rendering them incapable of reproducing.

Pedigree – The written record of a pedigreed dog's genealogy. Should extend to three or more generations.

Puppy – Any dog of less than 12 months of age.

Separation Anxiety – The anxiety and stress suffered by a dog left alone for any period of time.

Sire – The accepted term for the male parent.

Spay – The surgery to remove a female dog's ovaries to prevent conception.

Whelping – Term for the act of giving birth puppies.

Withers – The highest point of a dog's shoulders.

Wrinkle – Any folding and loose skin on the forehead and foreface of a dog.

Index

CPSIA information can be obtained at www.ICGtesting.com
Printed in the USA
LVOW07s0854040116

468993LV00009B/189/P